Your UDL Lesson Planner

Your UDL Lesson Planner

The Step-by-Step Guide
for Teaching All Learners

by

Patti Kelly Ralabate, Ed.D.

·P A U L·H·
BROOKES
PUBLISHING C⁰ ®

Baltimore • London • Sydney

Paul H. Brookes Publishing Co.
Post Office Box 10624
Baltimore, Maryland 21285-0624

www.brookespublishing.com

Typeset by Absolute Services, Baltimore, Maryland.
Manufactured in the United States of America by
Sheridan Books, Chelsea, Michigan.

Library of Congress Cataloging-in-Publication Data
The Library of Congress has cataloged the printed edition as follows:

Ralabate, Patti.
  Your UDL lesson planner : the step-by-step guide for teaching all learners / Patti Kelly Ralabate.
     pages   cm
  Includes bibliographical references and index
  Summary: "Through text and video, this book describes each UDL principle in depth for teachers to use the framework as they design instruction"—Provided by publisher.
     ISBN 978-1-68125-002-1 (paperback)—ISBN 978-1-68125-062-5 (pdf)—
     ISBN 978-1-68125-064-9 (epub)
     1. Lesson planning.   2. Inclusive education.   I. Title.

LB1027.4.R35 2016
371.3028—dc23   2015030128
British Library Cataloguing in Publication data are available from the British Library.

2020   2019   2018   2017

10   9   8   7   6   5   4   3   2

Contents

About the Videos and Downloadable Materials

Purchasers of the book may stream and view the accompanying videos for Chapters 1–6 and 8 for educational use. Purchasers may also download, print, and/or photocopy the blank forms from throughout the book. These materials are included with the print and e-book and are available at www.brookespublishing.com/downloads with (case sensitive) keycode: 72abPaK2b.

Videos

Video 1.1: Overview of 6 Steps of UDL Lesson Planning
Video 2.1: Defining Clear, Flexible, SMART Learning Goals
Video 3.1: Taking a Variability Perspective
Video 4.1: Selecting Accurate, Appropriate, and Meaningful Assessments
Video 5.1: Traditional Teaching Methods with a UDL Spin
Video 6.1: Choosing Materials and Media
Video 8.1: Using Self-reflection and UDL

Forms

Figure 1.3: UDL SWOT Analysis
Figure 2.2: Exercise Your Learning
Figure 3.5: Motivation Quiz—What Motivates You?
Figure 3.7: Representation Scramble Puzzle
Figure 4.1: Assessment Accessibility Checklist
Figure 5.2: Compare Teaching Methods and UDL Strategies
Figure 7.4: Check-In: Lesson Analysis
Figure 8.2: UDL Lesson Planning Expertise

About the Author

Patti Kelly Ralabate, Ed.D., universal design for learning (UDL) implementation expert and independent consultant, served as Director of Implementation for CAST and Director of the National Center on Universal Design for Learning. She was a UDL leadership fellow at Boston College and the National Education Association's key expert on special and gifted education in the Education Policy and Practice Department. She has authored, coauthored, or edited numerous guides and policy documents that serve as excellent resources for school personnel. Dr. Ralabate received a bachelor of science in education degree from the SUNY at Fredonia, New York, a master of arts in speech-language pathology from the University of Massachusetts, and a doctorate in special education from The George Washington University in Washington, D.C. She teaches as a part-time faculty member at The George Washington University.

Preface

Often, a series of experiences lead individuals to take a new course of action. In my case, there were four events that led to writing this book. The first occurred after I offered testimony to the Aspen Institute's Commission on No Child Left Behind on behalf of the National Education Association (NEA) regarding needed changes to the law's assessment and accountability provisions. Ricki Sabia, who was promoting alignment of Maryland's state policy and curriculum with universal design for learning (UDL), asked me to help share information about UDL with general education teachers. We joined with Mary Beth Klotz of the National Association of School Psychologists, Myrna Mandlawitz, a D.C. lobbyist for several education organizations, Nancy Reder of the National Association of State Directors of Special Education, and Lisa Thomas of the American Federation of Teachers, to establish the National UDL Task Force.

Together with the 40-plus organizations that became members of the task force, we advocated for the inclusion of UDL in federal legislation, such as the *Higher Education Opportunity Act of 2008*, which requires every teacher preparation program that receives federal funding to provide information about UDL to teacher candidates. Over the next few years, many of the National UDL Task Force member organizations created resources and shared information about UDL. As NEA Senior Policy Analyst for Special and Gifted/Talented Education, I did my part by working with the NEA IDEA Special Education Resource Cadre to create workshop materials and a policy brief on UDL. At this point, I viewed the UDL framework as a way to proactively provide *access* and eliminate barriers for learners.

Several years later, the second experience happened at a CAST workshop. I was honored to be a Boston College postdoctoral fellow in residence at CAST and was attending my first UDL workshop. As a speech-language pathologist, I connected the research basis of UDL with what I already knew about the neuropsychology of communication and learning. It made sense. I viewed UDL like a diagnostician would: it was helpful in planning for specific student learning *needs*. While Todd Rose described the predictability of learner variability, I experienced an "Aha!" moment. His explanation clarified that UDL defines how *all humans learn*. Consequently, I realized that because the UDL Guidelines are based on the neuroscience of learning, they not only offer a method of removing barriers but also provided a systematic, predictable way to *plan for each and every learner*. Designing video resources and writing articles to educate teachers about the predictability of learner variability became a key focus area.

The third experience occurred during a CAST UDL institute, but this time I was conducting the workshop with my CAST colleague, Allison Posey. I was quite focused on making sure that all the participants understood the potential impact that applying the UDL framework could have on meeting the learning needs of all students. One participant asked an obvious question: "How do you plan using UDL?" I recognized at that moment that educators need to know more than what the UDL framework is; they also need a process that will guide them through applying UDL to their lesson planning. With my CAST colleagues, I began to include more content on planning with UDL in our workshops and institutes.

A short time later, the fourth and final event occurred. My friend, Loui Lord Nelson, introduced me to her editor, Rebecca Lazo. Brookes Publishing had just published Loui's first book: *Design and Deliver: Planning and Teaching Using Universal Design for Learning*, and we were celebrating her success. Rebecca asked what book should be next, and I chimed in that we needed a text to guide educators through the lesson planning process using UDL. When she asked me if I would write it, I said yes. And, here we are.

Your UDL Lesson Planner: The Step-by-Step Guide to Teaching All Learners is the result of years of study focused on UDL and decades of working with amazing educators from all over who are eager to learn how to provide effective instruction for all learners. It is purposefully inclusive, offering examples of educators applying UDL at various school levels (e.g., early childhood, elementary, middle school, high school, college), teachers in a spectrum of fields (e.g., general and special education, related services, English as a second language, career and technical education, higher education), and lessons for a variety of subjects (e.g., English language arts, mathematics, social studies, science, library science, creative arts). In this way, I hope that you see yourself in the examples and find ideas and resources that you can immediately apply to your practice.

Acknowledgments

No one accomplishes important work without the guidance and support of others. This book would not be a reality without the inspirational research of David Rose and Anne Meyer and the thoughtful assistance of my fellow universal design for learning (UDL) travelers: Peggy Coyne, Rachel Currie-Rubin, Jenna Fournel, Austin Naughton, Allison Posey, Sharon Schultz, Nicole Tucker-Smith, Cynde Snider, and Joy Zabala.

In particular, thank you to Liz Berquist for her steadfast support and ground-breaking work on UDL implementation and Loui Lord Nelson for her unwavering friendship and *the* introduction that made things happen. Many thanks to the talented staff of Brookes Publishing and Center City Film and Video who made this endeavor fun and easy, especially my dedicated editor, Rebecca Lazo, and capable post producer, Jakkie Krinick. I want to also extend my deepest appreciation to the fabulous educators and students of the Cecil County Public Schools in Maryland who gave their time and talent to help us create the book's video exemplars: Associate Superintendent Carolyn Teigland, Gilpin Manor principal Catherine Dingle, Elkton Middle School principal Stuart Hutchinson, Rosalind Battee, Megan Law, Tammy Oyler, Britney Russell, Russell Sands, Kevin Skudalski, Tracey Varalli, and Christy Ward.

Finally, this book was a family venture. My everlasting gratitude to my wonderful husband and fellow educator, Sam, who critiqued chapters and volunteered to appear as an educator in the videos, and my extraordinary daughter, Kelly, who organized, narrated, and produced the book's professional-caliber videos. You two continue to be the wind at my back and beneath my wings.

1

Why Is Universal Design for Learning a Lesson Planning Process?

> This chapter introduces lesson planning based on the Universal Design for Learning (UDL) framework, describes multiple rationales for reading this book, and outlines how this book applies to UDL.

A veteran middle school teacher, Maria has seen many initiatives come and go without much lasting impact on her teaching, so she attends the latest district professional development day with lowered expectations. She often attends workshops with the best intentions: to find some "shiny new concept" to improve her teaching. Sometimes she picks up one or two new ideas to add to her repertoire, but usually no ground-shaking moment occurs. This time is different, however. This time she experiences what she later describes as her "Aha" moment. When the workshop presenter describes the UDL framework as a proactive instructional design process, Maria realizes that she hasn't examined her lesson planning in depth for many years. She thinks, Maybe UDL can make my teaching sparkle!

Maria's idea to make her teaching "sparkle" is one she shares with educators everywhere. Teachers want to experience the feeling of making a connection with that hard-to-reach student or ending a lesson with students eager for the next. There's nothing like that sense of accomplishment. Unfortunately, too many lessons are built on incorrect or old concepts about how students learn, or they are so constrained by stagnant formats that even the teachers who teach them are bored.

In his exploration of the "inner landscape of a teacher's life," Palmer states, "To educate is to guide students on an inner journey toward more truthful ways of seeing and being in the world" (1998, p. 6). He goes on to describe good teaching as more *process* than *product*. It is the process of envisioning, connecting, and reflecting that enables educators to concurrently rejoice in their daily work and hone their practice. That's where the UDL lesson planning process can help educators realize the sparkle that Maria yearns to feel.

 **Reflection**

How does Maria's "Aha" moment relate to your beliefs about your own instruction?

WHY READ THIS BOOK?

More and more educators are learning about UDL in their teacher preparation programs and at workshops, conferences, and professional development sessions. You may be reading this book as a course text, as a professional learning community (PLC) assignment, or for your own professional growth. In any case, you are among a growing cadre of educators across the United States and throughout the world who are exploring how to apply UDL to their instructional designs.

The goal of *Your UDL Lesson Planner: The Step-by-Step Guide for Teaching All Learners* is to support educators' efforts to change their practice, which this book does by walking readers through the step-by-step process of designing UDL lessons. In addition, this book models the UDL principles as its chapters guide you in creating UDL-infused lessons.

There are many reasons why educators are learning how to design lessons using the UDL framework, especially considering how classrooms today are changing.

Classes Are Becoming More Diverse

Often educators don't feel they have the appropriate preparation to meet the needs of all the students in their classes. Not only are PK–12 classrooms more diverse, but college classes are too.

Students with gifts and talents challenge educators to offer lessons to expand learning that goes beyond proficient expectations. English language learners are the fastest growing group within U.S. schools, and few educators have taken coursework to prepare those students or meet their unique needs. *UDL is a recommended approach to address academic and cultural diversity for a wide swath of learners* (Chita-Tegmark, Gravel, Serpa, Domings, & Rose, 2012).

> We inhabit a universe that is characterized by diversity.
>
> —Desmond Tutu

Classes Are Becoming More Inclusive

Although PK–12 and postsecondary classes are no longer as homogeneous as they once were and include many more students with disabilities, studies show that educators feel ill-equipped to include students with disabilities in general education classrooms (Schumm & Vaughn, 1995; Smith & Smith, 2000). UDL was originally conceptualized to provide more support in inclusive classes for students with significant needs (described by Meyer and Rose, 2005, as students "at the margins"). Yet research has demonstrated that once they are provided a description of UDL and a format to guide their planning, general and special education teachers can develop effective lesson designs that address the instructional needs of all their students, including students with disabilities (Courey, Tappe, Siker, & LePage, 2012; Spooner, Baker, Harris, Ahlgrim-Delzell, & Browder, 2007). *Educators have seen how lessons developed using the UDL framework meet the needs of all learners, including those with disabilities.*

Technology Offers Us More Flexibility than Ever Before

Flexibility is a critical aspect of lessons that meet the needs of all learners. Access to the Internet and digital-technology tools can make available a plethora of options for engaging learners and representing content as well as numerous applications learners can use to show what they're learning. However, you do not need digital technology or even an Internet connection to apply UDL to lesson planning (Novak, 2014)—but it can certainly help! *UDL lesson planning offers educators a guide for how to meaningfully apply technology to their instructional practice.*

Evaluation Systems Require Planning for All Learners

In this time of high-stakes education, educators need guidance on how to offer instruction that enables all learners to more fully meet state and local standards. Learning how to apply UDL to lesson design can inspire you to improve your skills and help you advance professionally (CAST & Danielson Group, 2014). *Teacher evaluation systems, such as those that are built on the Danielson Framework for Teaching, align closely with the UDL framework.*

 **Learning Link**

If you'd like to learn how UDL and the Danielson Framework for Teaching complement each other, check out the UDL–Danielson FfT Crosswalk at http://www.udlcenter.org/implementation/udl-danielson-crosswalk.

Learner Outcomes Offer a Focus

As Chapter 2 will describe in detail, it's important that learners know lesson goals and expected outcomes. In keeping with this critical aspect of lesson planning, readers of *Your UDL Lesson Planner* should know the learner outcomes that guide its content. Readers of this book will be able to

- Identify how they can integrate the UDL framework into lesson planning

- Apply UDL to specific, measurable, attainable, results-oriented, and time-bound (SMART) learning-goal development

- Develop flexible, accessible classroom assessments

- Employ a variety of ways to proactively embed the UDL framework in instructional methods

- Apply the UDL framework to make wise choices for lesson materials and media

- Find resources for infusing the UDL Guidelines and checkpoints in lesson designs

You may have decided to read this book to learn more about UDL, the lesson planning process, both, or for any of the reasons just mentioned. In any case, congratulations on taking this first step toward honing your practice!

WHY UDL?

Let's back up a minute. Before talking about UDL as a lesson planning process, let's clarify what UDL is. In the late 20th century, architects Ron Mace and colleagues conceived seven universal design (UD) principles that, when applied proactively to building design, result in structures that are accessible to all users and eliminate the need to retrofit buildings and products (Center for Universal Design, 2015). The UD principles remove physical barriers in the environment and help architects to meet the accessibility requirements of the Americans with Disabilities Act (ADA) of 1990 (PL 101-336).

In like fashion, CAST founders conceptualized UDL as a framework to help remove barriers in the learning environment. They adopted the term *universal design for learning* because UDL not only guides educators in designing lessons that are accessible but also helps them to create learning experiences that engage learners, activate thinking, and scaffold deep understanding. Nelson offers this clear explanation: "UDL is a framework that guides the shift from designing learning environments and lessons with potential barriers to designing barrier-free, instructionally rich learning environments and lessons" (2014, p. 2).

UDL is based on neuroscience research regarding how human beings learn. According to Meyer, Rose, and Gordon (2014), UDL is organized around three broad principles, which are aligned with three networks in the brain that involve the learning processes:

1. Multiple means for *engagement* of students (corresponding to the *affective* network—the *why* of learning)

2. Multiple means of *representation* of information to students (corresponding to the *recognition* network—the *what* of learning)

3. Multiple means for *action and expression* by students (corresponding to the *strategic* network—the *how* of learning)

Using the UDL principles, educators offer options for how students can engage in learning, receive information, and respond or demonstrate their knowledge and skills. Associated with each principle are a series of guidelines and checkpoints to help educators design instruction to meet the needs of students who exhibit the natural variability that exists in all classrooms (CAST, 2011). Figure 1.1 illustrates the UDL principles, guidelines, and checkpoints in a succinct visual graphic.

Meyer and colleagues (2014) explain that the framework embraces curriculum development that works for everyone—not a single, one-size-fits-all solution but rather flexible approaches that can be customized and adjusted to scaffold and support learning. Working under the false assumption that learners can be categorized as *typical* or *atypical,* educators have historically developed lessons that address the so-called average learner. Neuroscience clarifies that this was a false assumption, because the existence of an average learner is a myth. Although Chapter 3 will delve deeper into the concept of learner variability, it's important to emphasize this point: Each and every learner has unique strengths, skills, interests, desires, and readiness levels.

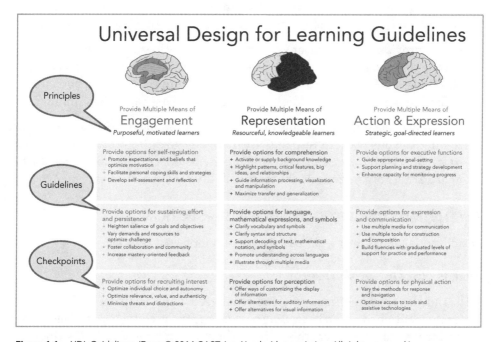

Figure 1.1. UDL Guidelines. (From © 2014 CAST, Inc. Used with permission. All rights reserved.)

Since no learner is exactly like any other and individuals learn in different ways, learning can be viewed as an interactive process that varies with each individual and each learning environment. As educators design lessons, the challenge is to offer the accessibility and support that each learner needs to gainfully interact with and learn from the curriculum in that particular learning environment. By infusing flexible options and multiple scaffolds and formats into lessons, teachers meet learner needs at the onset of instruction and have no need for retrofitting lessons that work for some but not for others. Using the UDL framework for lesson design creates lessons that work for *everyone*.

ORGANIZATION OF THE UDL GUIDELINES

Later in this book, I unpack the UDL Guidelines and each of the principles in depth as well as how to apply them to lesson designs. For now, let's explore some of the big ideas that undergird the UDL framework, starting with the structure of the framework. As previously stated, each principle suggests offering flexibility or multiple ways learners can engage in the learning environment in order to activate the corresponding brain network. Moreover, three guidelines further define each UDL principle. The guidelines, based on learning science research, represent how learning might predictably vary in any group of human beings (CAST, 2011; Meyer et al., 2014). Beneath each guideline are checkpoints that further refine how educators might address variability. Consider the following examples:

- As you provide multiple means of *engagement*—How are you going to gain learners' attention and interest? How are you going to keep them involved? How are you going to guide their motivation so that they want to learn more?

- As you provide multiple means of *representation*—How are you going to present the content so that it is accessible to every learner? How are you going to build meaning for new vocabulary? How are you going to connect new concepts with what learners already know in order to build deeper understanding?

- As you provide multiple means of *action and expression*—How are you going to offer various ways to respond? How are you going to provide scaffolding to learners with focused practice and precise feedback? How are you going to help learners organize and take responsibility for their own learning?

MYTHS, MISCONCEPTIONS, AND INTERSECTIONS

In addition to looking at what UDL is, let's explore what it is *not*.

UDL Is Not Universal Design

UDL and UD are sometimes used interchangeably, but they are different concepts. As mentioned at the beginning of this chapter, architects conceived seven UD principles to apply proactively to building design. The seven UD principles remove physical barriers in the environment and help architects to meet the accessibility requirements of the ADA. The UD principles are 1) equitable use, 2) flexibility in use, 3) simple and intuitive use, 4) perceptible information, 5) tolerance for error, 6) low physical effort, and 7) size and space for approach and use (Center for Universal Design, 2015).

Defined in the Assistive Technology Act of 1998 (PL 105-394), the UD principles guide the development of products, services, and environments to ensure access to people with the widest possible range of functional capabilities. Similar to UDL, the goal is to offer access from the outset to avoid costly or clumsy retrofitting. Both UDL and UD offer physical accessibility in education environments through multiple options for perception, but in addition, *UDL goes beyond accessibility by activating thinking, scaffolding deep understanding, and engaging learners.*

UDL Is Not Special Education

Sometimes people assume UDL applies exclusively to the field of special education. Special education is defined in federal statute as specially designed instruction that meets the unique needs of a student with a disability (Individuals with Disabilities Education Improvement Act of 2004 [PL 108-446]). It's true that both UDL and special education aim to create educational opportunities for students with disabilities. In fact, as mentioned earlier, UDL was originally conceived as a means of meeting the needs of students with significant disabilities; however, today *UDL is considered a framework that addresses the variability of all learners.*

UDL Is Not Technology Instruction

Educators wonder whether they must have technology, particularly digital technology, in order to implement UDL. In many schools, the technology specialists champion UDL because it offers educators a way to meaningfully and effectively use technology. So technology-instruction specialists may be the first to introduce teachers to the UDL framework as the specialists install new digital tools. The advantage of digital content is that it offers flexibility. With digital tools, text can be translated and transformed (e.g., text to speech, speech to text, text to American Sign Language, text to braille) and displayed onscreen and via multiple means (e.g., speech, graphics, video, animation, simulations). Digital technologies certainly make individualizing, customizing, and optimizing the learning experience easier.

Utilizing nondigital media may necessitate more time or organizational effort, but educators have extensive experience using nondigital technology. Educators, for example, have used chalkboards, display boards, projectors, audio and musical equipment, scales, and manipulatives in classrooms for decades. In fact, educators can and do implement UDL *unplugged,* thus successfully applying the UDL framework to lessons without digital technologies. The bottom line is: *Technology instruction is not the purpose for UDL implementation; it is a helpful means* (Rose, Gavel, & Domings, 2010).

UDL Is Not the Same as Differentiated Instruction

When first hearing about UDL, educators often ask, "Isn't UDL just differentiated instruction?" The answer is no. UDL and differentiated instruction (DI) have similarities, but they are not the same. Both aim to make learning accessible for all students, and like UDL, DI acknowledges that learners are unique. DI identifies learner aspects as interests, readiness, and a learner profile, which includes culture, gender, and environmental preferences. Both UDL and DI recommend that educators make instructional decisions to address learner differences, but DI emphasizes using formal and informal data for specific students as the basis for instruction. Teachers then select from a range of strategies to differentiate content, processes, products, or the learning environment in order for each student to acquire essential concepts, principles, and skills.

Implemented together, UDL and DI provide educators with myriad strategies to meet the needs of all students. For instance, you can use UDL as the overarching framework for lesson planning and then employ DI strategies for those students who need additional individualization.

A key contrast between DI and UDL is that DI emphasizes responding to individual needs, whereas *UDL emphasizes proactive design of the environment and instruction based on predictable, systematic learner variability.*

UDL Is Not a Checklist

First and foremost, UDL is not a simple checklist to scan through as you write your lesson plans. You may end up reviewing Figure 1.1 or a set of questions or ideas as you develop your lessons, but full implementation of the UDL framework requires that you think about your instruction differently. Like Maria, most UDL enthusiasts have experienced a similar "Aha" moment when they understand that UDL is a lens for examining curriculum and instructional design. A participant at a recent workshop described his "Aha" moment this way: "I started to feel like I was missing something that everyone else knew. Where is the checklist of things I need to do? Then it came to me: *UDL is not a checklist of things to do; it's a new* lens *for thinking about everything I do.*"

WHY REFER TO UDL AS A LESSON PLANNING PROCESS?

A framework can be defined as a structure or set of concepts, which certainly aligns with the workshop participant's description of UDL. UDL is a conceptual framework. In contrast, a process is a series of steps towards a goal or end. That definition certainly describes what teachers do as they design lessons, approaching planning in a sequential, step-by-step fashion. In this way, lesson planning *is* a process.

> Design is not just what it looks like and feels like. Design is how it works.
>
> Steve Jobs

As they've learned about UDL, educators have reported that they struggled when they tried to apply UDL to their lesson designs. They needed guidance about *how to do it,* particularly what to do first. They wondered what changes in their current planning processes would be most effective and efficient. They needed a *process* to follow.

That's what this book emphasizes: applying the UDL framework throughout the lesson planning process. What this book does not attempt to do is to offer a recipe for UDL. UDL is all about honoring individuality, flexibility, and choice. A recipe approach would entail specific tasks or ingredients required according to a lesson plan formula. Because learners are unique, teaching circumstances are different in various environments, and educators have enormous creativity, a single formula for lesson design that works for everyone is impractical.

One last point: Guskey (2002) proposed a model for viewing change in educators' beliefs and practices as aspects of a change process. He contended that effective, sustainable professional development is not attendance at a workshop but a continual process of growth that changes how educators think about their practice. It is my hope that as you apply the UDL framework to your lesson planning, you will discover that this process changes how you think about your teaching practice and how you view instruction.

HOW TO READ THIS BOOK

This book is organized according to a recommended sequence for developing a lesson—that is, defining goals; considering learner variability; determining assessments; deciding on methods, materials, and media; and teaching a lesson and then reflecting on it. You may choose to read this book chapter by chapter, from beginning to end, or in a different order that is more relevant to what you want to learn. The key point to keep in mind is that this book is intended as a guide available to use, reread, mark up, and add to as you enhance your application of UDL to your practice.

You may be reading this book as a course assignment or as a personal commitment to enhance understanding of UDL. In this case, digesting the book chapters in sequence will be most helpful, since each chapter is designed to build on the one before it. Or you may be reading this book as a shared learning task with a community of practitioners, such as a PLC. In this case, reading chapters out of sequence, applying the content, and then discussing observations with your PLC may be helpful. DuFour and Eaker (1998) emphasize the synergy that results when a group of staff members work together toward a shared outcome. Educators can learn much from collaborative lesson planning, mutual reflection, and observing one another teaching lessons that everyone designed together. In this way, taking this journey with others is likely to enhance learning.

WHAT ARE THE KEY FEATURES OF THIS BOOK?

This book is divided into eight chapters aligned with the six steps of the UDL lesson planning process, with two chapters describing how to choose methods and materials and an additional chapter that guides readers through building

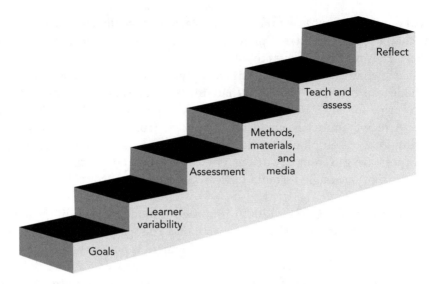

Figure 1.2.   UDL lesson planning process.

a lesson from beginning to end: 1) providing an overview of the UDL lesson planning process, 2) defining flexible and clear SMART goals, 3) considering learner variability, 4) determining appropriate assessments, 5) choosing methods, 6) selecting materials and media, 7) putting it all together in a lesson, and 8) refining learning through self-reflection. Figure 1.2 illustrates steps in the UDL lesson planning process, which build on one another.

Each chapter in this book is embedded with UDL features to aid learning:

- *To recruit interest and build relevancy and value,* each chapter begins with a brief scenario that describes a teacher who is learning about UDL and the lesson planning process.

- *To guide information processing and maximize learning transfer,* each chapter includes graphics or visuals, Take Note boxes that call out points worth remembering, and at least one exercise that readers can use to apply the new learning from that chapter.

- *To offer models, alternative representations, and provide options for comprehension,* each chapter includes examples and a video of real classroom teachers demonstrating the aspects of the UDL lesson planning process that is addressed in that chapter.

- *To monitor progress and offer mastery-oriented feedback,* each chapter includes a Check-in that readers can use to assess their learning from that chapter.

- *To support planning, strategy development, self-assessment, and reflection,* each chapter includes a Reflection question, relevant quotes, and opportunities to pause and think about relevant points.

- *To encourage further learning and support readers as "expert learners"* (i.e., knowledgeable, resourceful, motivated learners), each chapter includes suggested reflection questions and links to web sites and tools highlighted in Learning Link and Inspiration boxes, and the appendix includes an extensive list of resources and references.

SUMMARY

As educators like Maria learn about the UDL framework, they need resources that will guide them in applying it to their instructional practice. The goal of *Your UDL Lesson Planner: The Step-by-Step Guide for Teaching All Learners* is precisely that: to support efforts to change education practice by offering a step-by-step process for designing UDL lessons. There are numerous reasons for learning more about how to use the UDL framework in lesson design. Among these reasons are the realities of today's diverse classrooms and the expectation that all educators can and must be able to address the learning needs of all learners. Clearly describing the UDL framework debunks myths and misconceptions about it. In reality:

- The concept of universal design is related to UDL, but the principles are not the same.

- UDL benefits all students, not only those with disabilities.

- Digital technology provides helpful flexibility but is not necessary to implement UDL.

- Although differentiated instruction emphasizes responding to individual learning needs, UDL stresses instructional design that is proactive, based on systematic, predictable learner variability.

- UDL is not a checklist of things to do; it is a new lens or perspective on learning that impacts how educators plan instruction.

Your UDL Lesson Planner walks you through the six steps of the UDL lesson planning process: 1) defining flexible, clear SMART goals; 2) considering learner variability; 3) determining appropriate assessments; 4) selecting methods, materials, and media; 5) implementing a lesson plan; and 6) refining educator learning through self-reflection. Recognizing that educators are learners too, this book applies the UDL principles and guidelines through options and features that scaffold learning.

CHECK-IN

How Can UDL Lesson Planning Enhance Instruction?

Are you ready to dive deeper into UDL lesson planning? Since you've read the book this far, you probably are; however, before making changes to your lesson planning process to incorporate UDL, you may want to analyze its anticipated impact. A SWOT analysis (see Figure 1.3) will allow you to consider the potential strengths (S), weaknesses (W), opportunities (O), and threats (T) that changing your lesson planning practice may present.

UDL SWOT ANALYSIS

Strengths	Weaknesses
What are strengths of applying UDL to lesson planning?	What are potential weaknesses of applying UDL to lesson planning?

Opportunities	Threats
What opportunities does the UDL lesson planning process offer?	What potential threats exist that could negatively impact applying UDL to lesson planning?

Figure 1.3. UDL SWOT Analysis.

UDL LESSON PLANNING IN ACTION

We all learn differently. In addition to reading this chapter, you may want to see what UDL lesson planning looks like or view a UDL lesson in action. Go online to view Video 1.1: Overview of 6 Steps of UDL Lesson Planning (approximately 3 minutes; see the About the Videos and Downloadable Materials page for details) that offers an overview of the six steps of UDL lesson planning. In this video, you'll meet Maria, a middle school teacher who uses UDL as a lesson planning process to enhance her teaching. She understands that *UDL is a lens* for examining curriculum and designing instruction.

This video defines the UDL principles of engagement, representation, and action and expression and shows the six steps of the UDL lesson planning process in action. Look for examples of how to 1) focus students on a clear learning goal; 2) offer media as a scaffold to address learner variability; 3) embed formative assessments within lessons; 4) select methods, materials, and media that offer choice, activate background knowledge, and highlight critical understandings; 5) gather information about student learning during instruction; and (6) actively reflect on the effectiveness of your instruction.

REFLECTION QUESTIONS

1. Why do you think the UDL lesson planning process is the best way for you to plan lessons for diverse classrooms?

2. What would you have to change in order to apply UDL to your lesson planning process?

3. From what you've learned so far, how does the UDL lesson planning process differ from the lesson planning process you use now?

4. How might your assumptions about learning affect how you plan lessons?

2

Defining Learning Goals

A Critical First Step

This chapter explains how to create clearly defined learning goals, how to derive purpose and develop different types of learning goals based on content and performance standards, how to design flexible learning goals that recognize barriers in the learning environment and keep assessment in mind, and how important it is to share learning goals with learners.

When he heard that applying UDL to his lesson planning would allow him to hold all students to high expectations, Sam, a high school science teacher, was intrigued. Although he's proud that his instruction is based on the national science standards, he finds that nearly a third of his students aren't able to meet these expectations. He always designs his lessons with one learning goal for all the students. Sam doesn't like the idea of lowering expectations for some students and wonders if applying UDL to his lesson planning is a way to hold all students to high expectations while still providing the assistance that some students seem to need. But where does he start?

Like many educators, Sam's reluctance to lower expectations for some learners is a very real issue. It can be a challenge to define learning goals if teachers expect every student to achieve them. Wise educators know that creating learning goals that are standards based is more involved than just checking off which standards might be remotely connected to their content. Moreover, defining learning goals that take into consideration the learning needs of all students can be formidable for even the seasoned teacher.

FIRST STEP: CLEARLY DEFINED GOALS

To apply UDL to his lesson planning, Sam needs to start at the beginning with his lesson's goal. Building lessons that meet the needs of all students actually starts with defining clear learning goals. Why do your goals need to be clearly defined? Researchers have shown that learners can gain as many as 18 to 41 percentage points on assessments when teachers set and communicate clear goals for learning (Marzano, Pickering, & Pollock, 2001).

 **Reflection**

In what ways do you currently hold all learners to high expectations and still address their different strengths and challenges?

The purpose of a learning goal is "to offer direction to both the teacher and the students" (Nelson, 2014, p. 114). Precise, clearly defined learning goals allow you to build your instruction on what you want students to understand or be able to do by the completion of the lesson. Specific goals can also serve as motivators for learners, providing a clear understanding of the target knowledge or skills addressed in a lesson and offering guidance for how to be successful. Conversely, a lack of transparency in learning goals can result in ambiguity for you and your learners. Students will not be able to translate nonspecific or vague goals into desired actions. Likewise, you will not know if the students actually accomplished the task or learned the target knowledge or skills.

A veteran high school science teacher, Sam has files of lesson ideas and a closetful of materials he's organized by the science topics covered in the science textbook. For example, his lesson on the solar system is legendary, because the students have so much fun creating their models. They are obviously engaged and learning; however, Sam has started to feel that the lesson actually lacks focus and that the outcomes are unclear. Most of the content he includes on the unit test is covered in the text and only tangential to the lesson. He wonders, What's the purpose of this lesson?

Concentrate on Purpose, Not Activities

To define a clear learning goal, one must start with a clear purpose for the lesson. For far too long, teachers like Sam have focused their lessons on the *activity* of the lesson rather than its *purpose*. How do you identify your lesson's purpose? One approach to finding your lesson's purpose that works well with UDL is

Understanding by Design (UbD). In their landmark book, Wiggins and McTighe (1998) explain UbD as a conceptual approach to planning instruction that is focused on developing deep understanding. A teacher utilizes UbD to identify the purpose of his or her instruction by analyzing learning priorities related to the content—the "big ideas" and "enduring understandings" students should grasp. The authors recommend that teachers begin planning by first identifying what they want learners to know, understand, and be able to do by the end of a unit or lesson and then "backward design" from there. In other words, start by asking yourself, What is the point or purpose of this lesson?

Using a backward design approach, an educator does not view individual lessons as activities to *cover* the content. Instead, each lesson is a step toward a larger outcome, such as achieving the goals of the unit, attaining the course objectives for the semester, or meeting the curriculum standards for the year. In this way, meaningful, successful lessons link and build on one another.

 **Take Note**

See Pat's lesson in Chapter 7 (Figure 7.2) for an illustration of a lesson plan that applies the UDL framework to the UbD lesson structure.

Another way to define the purpose of a lesson is to unpack the performance or curriculum standards that are the basis of instruction, an idea discussed in more detail later in this chapter.

Design with the Assessment in Mind

The second task for the teacher is to decide what evidence is needed to show that the students actually learned the target knowledge or skills. Wise teachers use the assessments built into each lesson to hone the next assessment. Although Chapter 4 will delve deeper into assessment strategies to use in UDL lesson planning, it's essential to mention here how important it is for you to consider how you will evaluate attainment of the learning goal while you are developing the goal itself. If the learning goal points a lesson in the right direction, the assessment you use to measure achievement of the goal becomes a lens to help determine how close you're getting to the larger unit outcome or standard. Consequently, as you determine the purpose or goal of the lesson, also ask yourself, How will I know they learned it?

TYPES OF LEARNING GOALS

Learning goals focus on what students need to know or understand (*knowledge*) or what they need to be able to do (*skills*). In some cases, they also focus on attitudes or beliefs (*perceptions*). This is particularly relevant for lessons that require analysis. Note how these types of learning goals align with the UDL principles:

- Knowledge goals focus on the *what* of learning—recognition principle
- Skill goals focus on the *how* of learning—action and expression principle
- Perception or belief goals focus on the *why* of learning—engagement principle

Applying aspects of Bloom's Taxonomy, Marzano (2009) identifies four types of complexity to consider in developing learning goals:

- Retrieval—which includes recalling of information, locating, listing, and naming
- Comprehension—which includes translating, summarizing, demonstrating, and discussing
- Analysis—which includes identifying and analyzing patterns, organizing ideas, recognizing trends, composing, imagining, inferring, modifying, predicting, and combining
- Knowledge utilization—which includes problem solving, designing, experimenting, manipulating, comparing, evaluating, judging, recommending, and rating

Analysis and knowledge utilization goals focus on executive functioning, problem solving, and decision-making skills—including matching, classifying, analyzing errors, generalizing, and specifying or predicting. They require students to go beyond information that is available and to make inferences to create new understanding. Table 2.1 illustrates examples of how these four types of learning goals align with the UDL Guidelines.

> Education is not the filling of a pail, but the lighting of a fire.
> —William Butler Yeats

FLEXIBLE VERSUS CONSTRICTED LEARNING GOALS: YOU HAVE A CHOICE!

You have a critical choice to make when writing learning goals. You can develop learning goal statements that are flexible enough to allow all learners an opportunity to attain them *or* you can develop learning goal statements that are less flexible, therefore constricting how learners will achieve them. If writing goal statements that are constricted, you should also address what scaffolds you will need to include so that all learners will have the opportunity to achieve the learning goals.

Some have referred to this decision as determining whether or not to include the means in the goal statement. Let's unpack this concept. Many teachers have been taught to write goals that incorporate the means of determining the outcome within the learning goal statement itself. In this way, the goal is measurable. This is a good thing; however, a word of caution: Developing learning

Table 2.1.　Goal types linked with the UDL Guidelines

Type of complexity	Skills	UDL Guideline	Learning goals
Retrieval or recall	Recalling information Locating selected information Creating lists Naming	**Representation** Provide options for language, mathematical expressions, and symbols	Students will identify the key plot elements of Arnold Lobel's book *Frog and Toad Together.* After listening to L. Frank Baum's *The Wonderful Wizard of Oz,* students will describe the characters of Dorothy, Auntie Em, and Uncle Henry; the setting of the Kansan prairie; and major events, such as the arrival of the cyclone. Students will locate and determine the meaning of 10 specific academic vocabulary words (e.g., *crust, mantle, magma, lava*) from Seymour Simon's *Volcanoes.*
Comprehension	Translating Summarizing Demonstrating Discussing	**Representation** Provide options for comprehension Provide options for language, mathematical expressions, and symbols **Action and Expression** Provide options for expression and communication	Students will determine the main idea of *Holes* by Louis Sachar. Students will summarize the development of plot in Mark Twain's *Tom Sawyer.* Students will describe how Russell Freedman explains the beginning of the civil rights movement in his book *Freedom Walkers: The Story of the Montgomery Bus Boycott.*
Analysis (including synthesis)	Identifying patterns Analyzing patterns Organizing ideas Recognizing trends Composing Imagining or visualizing Inferring Modifying Predicting Combining information	**Action and Expression** Provide options for executive functions	Students will examine two objects with different weights, describe the difference, and predict which will rise and which will fall on a scale. Students will compose a lab report that identifies evidence from at least three relevant observations and their causes. Given a choice of media, students will analyze and express how and why individuals, events, or ideas develop and interact over the course of a fictional text.

(continued)

Table 2.1. *(continued)*

Type of complexity	Skills	UDL Guideline	Learning goals
Knowledge utilization or application	Problem solving Designing Experimenting Manipulating Comparing Evaluating Judging Recommending Rating	**Action and Expression** Provide options for expression and communication Provide options for executive functions	Students will evaluate a speaker's point of view, reasoning, and use of evidence to determine how accurate the argument is on a four-point scale. Given a choice of media, students will solve real-world mathematical problems involving perimeters of polygons.

goals that are inflexible or constricted can lead to rigid lessons in which you leave little room for offering options to your learners. This inflexibility can result in a significant portion of a class failing to accomplish the learning goal. For example, consider the learning goal that Emma developed for her lesson: *Students will* write *the meaning of 20 selected vocabulary words as they are used in* Charlotte's Web.

The purpose of Emma's lesson is to teach students how to use a fictional text to derive the meaning of at least 20 vocabulary words. This is a vital skill for students to learn; however, by requiring students to write the vocabulary word definitions, Emma's learning goal unnecessarily complicates and constricts how students will show that they understand the word meanings. Those learners who have difficulty with writing may be able to find the word definitions but will experience an additional burden or barrier to achieving the learning goal. Unless a specific means (production type) is required (i.e., writing), learning goals should be unrestricted by the means learners use to achieve the outcome. Let's reconsider the learning goal for Emma's lesson using a more flexible verb: Students will *describe* the meaning of 20 selected vocabulary words as they are used in *Charlotte's Web.*

By substituting a flexible action verb (i.e., describe) for a more constricted one (i.e., write), Emma now has a learning goal that a wider margin of learners can achieve, even those for whom writing is laborious (e.g., English language learners, students with writing difficulties) and those with physical limitations who cannot write.

 **Take Note**

To help you to consider more flexible verbs for your learning goals, Table 2.2 includes 100 action verbs you can use to write learning goals that are specific and measureable.

Table 2.2. One hundred active verbs for writing specific, measurable goals

add	demonstrate	follow directions	propose
analyze	describe	formulate	question
apply	design	identify	read
appraise	detect	illustrate	recall
arrange	determine	imitate	recognize
assemble	develop	indicate	reconstruct
calculate	devise	infer	record
categorize	diagnose	initiate	relate
choose	diagram	inspect	repeat
cite	differentiate	interact	report
collect	differentiate between	interpret	respond
communicate	discriminate	list	restate
compare	discuss	locate	review
complete	distinguish	manage	select
compose	divide	modify	sequence
conclude	dramatize	multiply	solve
construct	draw conclusions	name	spell
contrast	employ	operate	state
correlate	engage in	organize	subtract
copy	estimate	pick	tell
create	evaluate	plan	translate
criticize	examine	predict	underline
debate	experiment	prepare	use
deduce	explain	present	utilize
define	express	produce	write

From Ralabate, P.K. (2010). *Meeting the challenge: Special education tools that work for all kids.* Washington, DC: National Education Association; adapted by permission.

LEARNING GOALS THAT RECOGNIZE BARRIERS

Although it's preferable to use a flexible verb in your goal statement, it is sometimes necessary to develop learning goals that include specific, definitive actions because teaching that skill *is* the purpose of the lesson. For instance, if the lesson is focused on teaching reading, writing, speaking, or applying a mathematical operation, you'll need to use the appropriate verb representing that skill or task in your learning goal statement. As a result, the goal statement will contain a constricted verb.

Of course, in this instance the choice is still yours. If you must use a less flexible verb or your curriculum requires you to use a constrictive verb in your learning goal statement, you can choose to include the scaffolds necessary for those learners who will experience barriers in achieving the desired outcome. In summary, your choice is to either 1) write a learning goal with a flexible verb or 2) write a learning goal with a constricted verb and include scaffolds within the goal statement that will allow all learners the opportunity to achieve it.

Scaffolds are temporary aids or assistance to guide students in reaching the goal. Chapter 6 includes a robust discussion of scaffolds, but a simple rule of thumb for developing learning goals that reflect scaffolding options is to add a clause to your learning goal statement that describes use of the scaffold. For example, the following learning goal statement illustrates a learning goal that includes a scaffolding strategy: Using a written summarization strategy illustrating a series of reduction principles and a graphic organizer as needed, students will *write* at least one paragraph explaining how key details in the text support at least two main ideas of the text.

Some researchers suggest that educators level learning goals based on their perceptions of learners' competence. Simply put, a few authors recommend developing several distinct goals for different students, or groups of students, representing various desired outcomes for the same lesson. Remember that Sam, the science teacher, doesn't like this idea. He has a very good reason: This practice invariably lowers expectations for some students. It is also usually unnecessary if you thoughtfully write learning goals with flexible verbs and incorporate scaffolding strategies into your goal statement when your outcomes focus on constricted or less flexible actions.

STANDARDS PROVIDE PURPOSE

Today most lessons in public school classrooms across the United States address state or local content standards or performance objectives. The most widely known student standards are the Common Core State Standards (CCSS), which the National Governors Association and the Council of Chief State School Officers initiated in June 2009. So far, 42 states and the District of Columbia have adopted the CCSS for English language arts and mathematics.

 **Learning Link**

To learn more about the intersection of the CCSS and UDL, see the National Center on UDL crosswalk at http://www.udlcenter.org/implementation/udl_ccss.

Many elementary educators are required to align their lessons to the CCSS or other student performance standards that their state or school has adopted. They are not alone. College faculty and postsecondary instructors similarly are often required to incorporate specific career-oriented standards into their course syllabi and subsequent class sessions. For instance, institutions of higher learning that are seeking accreditation for their programs from national professional organizations (e.g., the American Speech–Hearing–Language Association, the Council for the Accreditation of Educator Preparation) must demonstrate that the courses they offer will prepare students to meet specific career expectations. Even some private school educators must construct their lessons based on curriculum or content standards their school leadership approves.

Look for purpose. You'll recall that Sam loved teaching his solar system lesson but was beginning to wonder what the point of the lesson was. He knew he could base his learning goal on the earth and space science (ESS) standards from the Next Generation Science Standards (2013); however, he was uncertain about how to write learning goals based on standards.

> Efforts and courage are not enough without purpose and direction.
>
> —John F. Kennedy

Let's investigate how Sam could align his solar system lesson with the specific science standards. Here is an ESS standard related to Sam's solar system modeling lesson: "Develop a model based on evidence to illustrate the life span of the sun and the role of nuclear fusion in the sun's core to release energy in the form of radiation" (ESS1.A).

First, Sam must examine what the standard is requiring his learners to know and be able to do—What is its core purpose? To extract which essential knowledge or skills will become the lesson's core purpose from the standard, Sam considers the following questions:

- What content knowledge is at the center of this standard? (Remember that content knowledge is more than facts. It also includes concepts, big ideas, principles, and important understandings.)

- How will this lesson add to and build on previous lessons?

- What background knowledge do learners have or need?

- What skills are necessary to accomplish the tasks embedded in this standard?

- If learners will be introduced to a new concept or skill, is one lesson time-period sufficient, or should this content be phased in or staged over multiple lessons?

Sam realizes that the standard he is teaching toward focuses on an activity (i.e., developing a model) and the content knowledge students need to create an accurate representation (i.e., the role of nuclear fusion in the sun's release of energy). Developing the model is not the desired learning; it is the way the students will show their understanding. Analyzing the standard in this way leads Sam toward a goal for his lesson. The standard therefore serves as a basis for his learning goal, but it is not the learning goal itself. Instead, the learning goal addresses the real purpose of the lesson: to build core knowledge about the sun. An example of a clearly defined learning goal for Sam's lesson could be: Students will *analyze* data from selected informational texts to create a three-dimensional illustration of how the sun's release of energy affects the earth and other planets in our solar system.

This learning goal is more involved than just building a model. It requires students to identify data related to the sun's release of energy from informational texts, such as the science text or supplemental articles; to organize, analyze, and synthesize the information in a manner that forms the conceptual and structural basis for the three-dimensional illustration; to determine a process for constructing the illustration; and then to build the model using all of this information. In reality, creating the three-dimensional model of the solar system may be the culmination of several lessons that build a deep understanding of the sun and solar system.

CONTENT VERSUS PERFORMANCE STANDARDS

Not all standards are alike. Broad statements that describe content areas students should understand at specific grade levels are *content standards*. They can also be called *curriculum standards* or *subject standards*. These define the concepts, knowledge, or information that is important to know within each academic discipline. For example, Annabella wants to design a UDL lesson for her second-grade class to address the following mathematics content standard: "Measure the length of an object by selecting and using appropriate tools such as rulers, yardsticks, meter sticks, and measuring tapes" (CCSS.Math.Content.2.MD.A.1).

To achieve this content standard, her learners will need to make sense of numerical quantities, manipulate mathematical symbols, understand the process of measurement, and be able to use appropriate tools in a strategic way. Her learning goal actually addresses several of these concepts: Using the appropriate measuring tools, students will *determine* the length of various animals described in *Actual Size* by Steven Jenkins and *report* their measurements to the class recorder for class tallying.

Annabella's learning goal builds background knowledge by linking the concept of measurement with appropriate reading content. And, because it incorporates two flexible verbs (i.e., *determine* and *report*), the goal allows multiple means of student engagement and expression. It also permits different students to fulfill various roles. For instance, the mathematically advanced student can serve as the class recorder, who adds the students' measurements for the class.

In contrast to broader content standards, *performance standards* measure how well a learner meets the content standard. A performance standard often has levels (e.g., 4, 3, 2, 1 or advanced, proficient, novice, basic) or is stated as an absolute. The following is a second-grade performance standard from the Common Core Georgia Performance Standards framework: "Fluently *add* and *subtract* within 20 using mental strategies. By end of Grade 2, know from memory all sums of two one-digit numbers" (MCC.2.OA.2).

As you can see, a performance standard is a specific expectation that includes a definite product or performance level. If you are developing UDL lessons based on performance standards, you may need to use constricted verbs but can also build scaffolds into your learning goal that will assist your students in achieving the standard during your lesson. For instance, a learning goal that includes scaffolds for the performance standard just mentioned could be expressed in this way: Using a number line and manipulatives as needed, students will *add* at least 10 sets of two one-digit numbers.

The number line and manipulatives are scaffolding strategies that can be available for those students who need them to build the mathematical mental strategies. Although a few students may always need them, you can fade out the scaffolding strategies over time as most of your learners become more confident and independent.

Take Note

To help you recognize those constricted verbs that may need scaffolding, Table 2.3 illustrates flexible and constricted action verbs organized by subject area.

Table 2.3. Examples of verbs to address specific standards

English language arts—flexible verbs		
	Choose	Explain
	Cite	Express
	Clarify	Judge
	Communicate	Identify
	Compose	Indicate
	Construct	Interpret
	Convey	Pick
	Correct	Present
	Create	Produce
	Defend	Recognize
	Define	Reveal
	Describe	Revise
	Devise	Select
	Display	Share
	Distinguish	Show
	Exhibit	Specify
English language arts—constricted verbs		
	Articulate	Read
	Decode	Say
	Mark	Speak
	Name	State
	Orate	Take
	Outline	Talk
	Point	Transcribe
	Pronounce	Write
	Recite	
Mathematics—flexible verbs		
	Analyze	Demonstrate
	Answer	Determine
	Apply	Equate
	Apportion	Explain
	Calculate	Explicate
	Combine	Formulate
	Compare	Illustrate
	Compute	Predict
	Decipher	Prove
	Decrease	Solve
	Deduce	Tally
Mathematics—constricted verbs		
	Add	Graph
	Copy	Multiply
	Diagram	Replicate
	Divide	Subtract
	Draw	

WHAT'S SO SMART ABOUT SMART GOALS?

Effective learning goals should pass the SMART test. In case this is the first time you've heard about SMART goal design, here is a brief explanation. The SMART acronym, which George Doran originally presented to business managers in 1981, has recently found its way into education circles. Various districts and state departments of education have adopted the concept behind the acronym and are offering professional learning on how to write SMART goals. Sometimes different words are used to define a few of the acronym's letters, but the following descriptions are most often used by educators:

S—*specific to a student-based outcome:* The learning goal should clearly state what you expect students to know or be able to do as the outcome of the lesson. As outlined earlier in this chapter, goals that describe completing an activity or that use vague verbs are not specific.

M—*measureable by providing timely evidence:* In most cases, the assessment should be defined in the learning goal statement, and it should provide you with ongoing data or evidence that learning is improving. Goals that are tied to end-of-year assessments or standardized tests do not provide ongoing evidence that learners are achieving the learning targets, so it's best to use rubrics and formative assessments for measuring goal achievement. Chapter 4 will expand on this idea.

A—*attainable by all students within a reasonable time frame:* Learning goals need to consider the readiness of all learners to move forward. If students cannot achieve learning goals within the time frame of the lesson, those who are struggling can be overlooked. Here's where scaffolding can help you develop goals that all the learners in your classroom or learning environment can achieve. Also, if your goals hold students to unrealistic, absolute levels of achievement or do not account for learner variability, they may prove to be demotivating to you and your students. Chapter 3 will expand on this concept.

R—*results oriented, yielding student-based learning:* Learning goals need to be learner focused. Learning goals that define what the teacher will do during the lesson do not result in student outcomes.

T—*time bound and regularly measured:* You should define learning goals for accomplishment within a specific time frame and assess them via regular observation and checks for understanding. Moreover, the needs of your learners—not artificial or tangential constraints, such as scripted curriculum or administrative pacing decisions—should drive time for accomplishment.

Table 2.4 illustrates examples of flexible, SMART goals.

SHARING LEARNING GOALS WITH LEARNERS

Research shows that learners are more successful and engaged in learning when they know the learning goals they are expected to achieve (Brophy, 2001).

Table 2.4. Examples of flexible, SMART learning goals

Content and grade level	Flexible, SMART goals (italics indicate core learning goal statement)
Preschool (birth–5)	With prompting as needed, *students will recall key details from a familiar nursery rhyme to answer four out of five who and what questions* (based on 2013 New Jersey State Department of Education Preschool Teaching and Learning Standards, RL.PK.1).
English language arts elementary (K–5)	After the teacher shares/reads [name of book] with/to the class, *students will describe at least two main characters, the setting, and at least three major story events* either using a graphic organizer or via report to a peer partner (based on CCSS.RL.1.3).
	Students will compose a first-draft opinion piece on [topic] supporting a point of view with at least two reasons (based on CCSS.W.3.1).
English language arts middle school (6–8)	*Students will analyze how Longfellow's poem "Paul Revere's Ride" uses descriptive words and phrases to create a theme of urgency and speed in Revere's ride and express their conclusions* (at least at a proficient level as measured by a presentation rubric) *in a short (3-minute) presentation using media* (e.g., slides, video, paper) *of their choosing* (based on CCSS.ELA-Literacy.RL.6.5).
English language arts high school (9–12)	Given a checklist and choice of topics, *students will conduct searches and gather relevant information from at least three authoritative print and digital sources* [in preparation for producing a written assignment comparing and contrasting the differences between fictional and nonfictional books focused on the same topic] (based on CCSS.ELA-Literacy.WHST.9–10.8).
Mathematics (K–5)	*Students will determine whether a group of objects (up to 20) has an even number of members, devise an equation to express the even number as a sum of two equal addends, and show their answers,* using a provided worksheet or digital format, with 80% accuracy (based on CCSS.Math.Content.2.OA.C3).
Mathematics (6–8)	Given story examples involving tipping at a restaurant, *students will use proportional relationships to solve 10 multistep word problems on percents and report their responses* to peer work partners to add to the class gratuity scale representation (based on CCSS.Math.Content.7.RP.A.3).
Mathematics (9–12)	*Students will use data from a student survey to estimate the mean for at least 10 selected questions and report their answers* via the class wiki with at least 90% accuracy (based on CCSS.Math.Content.HSS.IC.B.4).
World language	Using a [insert language, such as Spanish or Japanese] conversation guide, *students will engage in 10-minute proficient or higher level small-group discussions related to shopping at a grocery store for elements of a dinner meal* as measured by the spoken language rubic (based on National Standards for Foreign Language Education, Standard 1.2).
Science	Given examples of how the surface of the earth changes due to slow processes, such as erosion and weathering, and rapid processes, such as landslides, volcanic eruptions, and earthquakes, *students will correctly respond to at least 8 out of 10 exit ticket questions* (based on Next Generation Science Standards, 4-ESS3-2).

(continued)

Table 2.4.   *(continued)*

Content and grade level	Flexible, SMART goals (italics indicate core learning goal statement)
Social studies	Using information from our text and secondary sources, *students will record data on world maps to track the spread of the black death (bubonic plague) as it was carried westward from Asia to Africa and Europe* at a proficient or higher level, as measured by a rubric on mapping skills (based on New York State 9–12 Social Studies Framework, 2013).
Physical education	Given verbal and visual examples, *students will identify with 90% accuracy at least five physical and psychological changes that result from participation in a variety of physical activities* (based on National Physical Education Standard 5).
Music	*Students will sing with expression and good breath control throughout their singing ranges in small ensembles* at a proficient or higher level, as measured by a singing rubric, over three class periods (based on National Association for Music Education Performance Standards, Grades 5–8, Standard 1).
Art	With prompting and encouragement, *students will create an individual work of art using modeling clay* at a proficient or higher level, as measured by an observational checklist, over two class periods (based on National Arts Standards, VA:Cr2.1.7a).
Library	*Students will seek information using a variety of formats to answer a list of questions generated based on a personal interest,* as measured by a student self-assessment checklist (based on American Library Association Standards for the 21st-Century Learner, 4.2.2).
Career tech	*Students will apply the principles of* [name career technical skill] *at a proficient or higher level to solve problems presented in a workplace situation as measured by a teacher observation scale* (based on the Common Career Technical Core by NASDCTEc, 2012).

It can be a motivating factor that guides students' development of self-regulation skills. Thus, the first step in engaging your learners as self-directed learners is sharing the learning goals with them. You can do this by posting the learning goals in your classroom or learning environment, reviewing the goals at the beginning of the lesson, asking students to restate the learning goal in their own words, asking students to check on their own progress during the lesson, and reviewing the learning goals at the end of the lesson as part of the lesson summary.

 **Inspiration**

This video demonstrates a simple choral response strategy for clarifying goals. Students repeat SWBAT (pronounced *Swabat*), which stands for *students will be able to,* followed by the learning goal: https://www.teachingchannel.org/videos/making-lesson-objectives-clear.

Figure 2.1. Speak cartoon. (From Flanagan, M. [n.d.] Speak dog comic. Retrieved from www.cartoonstock.com; reprinted with permission.)

Providing students with an opportunity to develop the learning goals is another great technique. Some teachers don't view this as an efficient or appropriate endeavor for every lesson, however. Another excellent strategy is to ask learners to establish their own personal learning goals once you offer the overarching learning goals at the beginning of the lesson. In this way, the lesson becomes more relevant for them, as they generate their own connections to it.

Writing Individual Education Program Goals with a UDL Lens

If you are a special educator or specialized instructional support professional, such as a speech-language pathologist or occupational therapist, it is likely that you will be writing learning goals that address your students' individual education program (IEP) goals. As a matter of fact, some states and school districts require IEP goals to be written as SMART goals. Note that the focus of this book is on developing lessons, not IEPs; however, it will be easier to address your students' IEP goals in various learning environments—including the general education classroom—if you keep in the mind the discussion in this chapter regarding use of flexible rather than constricted verbs when you are constructing IEP goals. In addition, IEP goals that reflect the flexibility of the UDL framework allow for increased collaboration opportunities between you and your colleagues in general education classrooms.

 **Learning Link**

To read about how a general education teacher and speech-language pathologist used UDL as a base for collaborative planning, see Ralabate, Currie-Rubin, Boucher, and Bartecchi (2014), http://www.cast.org/our-work/publications/2014/collaborative-planning-udl-speech-language-pathologists-ralabate.html#.WTv2rrpFwr0.

SUMMARY

Let's recap: The first step in the UDL lesson planning process is to develop a clearly defined, measurable learning goal. Start by asking yourself, What is the point or purpose of this lesson? The purpose of the lesson is not to cover the content or to complete the activity. Instead, you can derive the purpose of your lesson from the content or performance standards that apply to your discipline or subject matter. Learning goals focus on what students need to know or understand (*knowledge*), what they need to able to do (*skills*), or their attitudes and beliefs (*perceptions*). Effective learning goals should be SMART goals: specific, measurable, attainable, results oriented, and time bound. To build learner engagement, be sure to share the learning goal with your students. Think about taking a backward design approach so that each lesson's goal relates to the next lesson in a coordinated manner to build the big ideas or knowledge and skills that you've identified as important for your students. As you develop your learning goal, ask yourself, How will I know they learned it? The answer to this question leads to your lesson assessment. Finally, state the purpose of the lesson in a clear, well-defined learning goal that either 1) uses a flexible verb to allow your students multiple ways to accomplish the goal (see Figure 2.2) or 2) includes scaffolding strategies that assist students who experience difficulty achieving the goal. Once you define the desired knowledge, skills, and/or perceptions in the learning goal, you can design the learning experience by determining the assessment, methods, materials, and media for the lesson.

CHECK-IN
10 Questions to Ask About Your Learning Goals

- Are your learners clear about the purpose of your lesson?

- To what extent are your goals flexible?

- To what extent are your goals rigorous?

- How meaningful and relevant are your goals?

- How much scaffolding do you need to include in your goal statements to meet the needs of all learners?

- How are you involving learners in personal goal setting?

- How do your goals allow for student choice?

- How do your goals guide students to successfully achieve them?

- To what extent are your goals aligned with critical standards?

- How SMART are your learning goals?

UDL LESSON PLANNING IN ACTION

In addition to reading this chapter, you may want to view a video (approximately 3 minutes in length) that offers a brief window into the first step in the

Exercise Your Learning

DIRECTIONS: Use flexible verbs and the SMART goal descriptions to make the following learning goals smarter and flexible.

Examples of goals	What's not so SMART or flexible?	Flexible and SMARTer goals
The teacher will use visual brainstorming techniques to help students generate ideas, record what they know about the Holocaust, and identify questions for further inquiry.	❑ Not flexible ❑ Not specific ❑ Not measureable ❑ Not attainable ❑ Not results oriented ❑ Not time bound	
All learners will understand numbers 11 through 19 as 10 plus some ones.	❑ Not flexible ❑ Not specific ❑ Not measureable ❑ Not attainable ❑ Not results oriented ❑ Not time bound	
Students will analyze a primary source to better understand the creator's perspective and the time period in which he or she lived.	❑ Not flexible ❑ Not specific ❑ Not measureable ❑ Not attainable ❑ Not results oriented ❑ Not time bound	
Students will become familiar with the library database and how to extract information from it to best answer their created questions.	❑ Not flexible ❑ Not specific ❑ Not measureable ❑ Not attainable ❑ Not results oriented ❑ Not time bound	
Learners will recall and write definitions for 20 vocabulary words.	❑ Not flexible ❑ Not specific ❑ Not measureable ❑ Not attainable ❑ Not results oriented ❑ Not time bound	

Figure 2.2. Exercise Your Learning.

UDL lesson planning process: defining clear, flexible, SMART learning goals. (See Video 2.1: Defining Clear, Flexible, SMART Learning Goals [go online to see the video].) You'll meet Sam, a high school science teacher who starts applying UDL to his lesson planning by developing learning goals with flexible verbs that provide for student choice. For example, to allow all learners to be successful, including those who struggle with writing, Sam defines a learning goal for his solar system lesson that asks students to *create a model* rather than *write a description*.

This video demonstrates how educators 1) identify the purpose of their lessons using achievement or curriculum standards, 2) build choice into their lessons by defining learning goals that use flexible verbs, and 3) design learning goals that pass the SMART test. You'll observe a teacher sharing learning goals with learners using a SWBAT call-and-response technique. The teacher posts the lesson's learning goal, reads it at the beginning of the lesson, and asks students to restate it. Finally, you'll see students checking their own progress during the lesson and reviewing their learning goals at the end of the lesson.

REFLECTION QUESTIONS

1. Why is it preferable to inform learners of the learning goals? In what ways do teachers and learners benefit? Are there any disadvantages?

2. In what way do standards direct your lesson plans now? How do you see standards-based learning goals affecting your instruction?

3. To what extent can learning goals that incorporate flexible verbs make a difference for you and your learners?

4. How can utilizing SMART goals make your instruction more effective?

3

Taking a Variability Perspective

This chapter explains how teacher perspectives affect lesson planning, what the terms *learning* and *expert learning* mean, how the brain processes novel information, and how to apply the concept of learner variability to UDL lesson planning.

After teaching at a liberal arts college for 15 years, Professor Brian O'Malley is in a comfortable situation. He's achieved tenure, teaches the same four to five courses each year, and has plenty of research and writing opportunities; yet he's beginning to feel a bit like the legendary fictional professor Charles Kingsfield (portrayed by John Houseman) from The Paper Chase, *the 1978 television show about Harvard Law School. Like Kingsfield, Brian primarily lectures and often relies on whole-class queries that many of his students nervously struggle to answer. Each semester his classes have some stars and a couple of slackers, and the rest of the students fall somewhere in the middle, closely representing the typical bell curve distribution. Growing uneasy with his teaching approach, Brian decides to explore UDL after an introductory overview of the framework at a recent faculty meeting. He contemplates applying a few UDL strategies to his planning and then has a realization: First, I may need to take a different view of my students. They are far more variable than I thought. Maybe my bell curve perspective needs to change.*

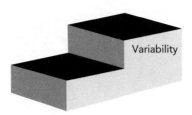

For Brian, changing his perspective on his students is a vital step toward improving his instructional practice. This may be the case for you too. Often educators who are concerned about meeting the varied learning demands of their students attempt employing numerous strategies they discover at workshops or through discussions with colleagues. They may feel liberated by their efforts to eclectically try different tactics in reaction to student needs, but ultimately a sense of disappointment with the results sets in. One UDL expert from Indiana, George Van Horn, refers to this approach as applying "random acts of excellence." Rooted in the concept of systematic, predictable learner variability, the UDL framework provides educators like Brian with both a new view of student learning and intentional strategies to plan for it. Let's explore what *taking a variability perspective* for student learning means.

 **Reflection**

Think about how you currently address learner variability in your lesson planning process and write down three strategies. How closely do they align with the UDL Guidelines?

PERSPECTIVES IMPACT INSTRUCTION

Although educators have recognized since antiquity that learners vary in numerous ways, teaching approaches haven't addressed those differences successfully. Taking a quick look at the history of instructional pedagogy helps to make this point: Over the centuries, instructional strategies changed based on the view of student learning that was prevalent at the time (Molenda, 2012). Prior to the 19th century, when formal education was primarily for the wealthy, teachers offered individual instruction to encourage each student's individual growth. With the advent of public education for the masses in the 19th and early 20th centuries, group-paced instruction became a common focus of educators across the United States.

In the mid-20th century, however, things started to change with the acceptance of Bloom's Taxonomy. With this change in philosophy, teachers began to put aside rote memorization techniques and pacing in favor of promoting increased levels of knowledge acquisition for every student through a mastery learning approach. Then in the late 20th century, psychologists proposed the bell curve premise, suggesting that any group of students predictably consists of a few (i.e., 5%) who perform at the top of the class, a few (i.e., 5%) who perform at the bottom, and the rest, who perform somewhere in between with the bulk in the very middle. They represented their statistics in a bell shape, such as the one in Figure 3.1—the basis of Brian's current bell curve perspective of his learners.

Perspectives Guide Planning

Central to all of historical instructional approaches is how educators view learners and the learning process. International education authorities such as Hargreaves and Fullan (1992) suggest that if teachers plan lessons that "teach to the middle" or expect some learners to fail, these expectations unconsciously become self-fulfilling prophecies. In other words, if Brian believes a few students are likely to fail his course, then he plans instruction to address the learning of the students in the middle or above, and those students are indeed the ones who perform at mid-range or above. The others rarely surprise him.

More recently, Hargreaves and Fullan (2012) argued that no matter how much schools insist they do otherwise, most schools still plan for students as if they were all the same. Let's pause for a second. Do you agree? Think about how your school is set up. Are most, if not all, of the students studying the same coursework or curriculum content and using the same textbooks? Are teachers primarily delivering content to everyone at the same time and in the same way? Is there a prevailing assumption that not all learners are competent—that some are not able to learn and will fail? If you're saying yes to these questions and you're interested in changing this situation for your learners, the UDL framework will offer you a new perspective on learning that will help you meet the varied needs of all your students.

What Does *All* Mean?

Let's think about a question I sometimes hear: Which learners benefit from UDL lesson planning? The answer to this question is, simply put: *All* learners benefit! It's true that CAST founders first conceptualized UDL as a curriculum design

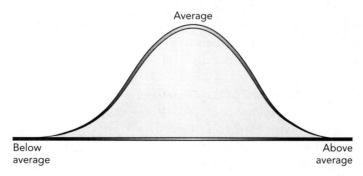

Figure 3.1.   Illustration of a bell curve.

framework that could redesign K–12 general education classrooms to be more meaningfully inclusive and conducive for students with significant disabilities; but that disposition evolved quickly, as UDL originators saw how well the framework helped educators create learning environments to address the learning needs of *all* learners. *All* applies to students who are viewed as gifted learners as well as those who typically struggle to learn the simplest academics, the youngest learners as well as adult learners. In fact, *all* includes you!

The UDL Framework: Not Another Way to Categorize Learners

Human beings seem to have a propensity for sorting and labeling their environment. In *The Forgotten Dream of American Public Education,* author Robert Bullough describes how schools tend to categorize learners in order to meet their perceived *needs.* He goes on to explain what he calls the "fundamental tension" between the typical definition of the word *needs* and how school staff use it:

> Needs are almost always understood as lacks—the task is to find out what a young person cannot do, when he or she is supposed to be able to do it, as determined by a statistical norm, like a grade level. In the name of meeting student needs, young people are categorized and placed in programs that offer widely differing opportunities to become educated; it is all done for the love of children and in the knowledge of what is best for them. (1998, pp. 38–39)

Looking at the types of labels in education (e.g., nondisabled versus disabled, typical versus atypical, regular versus special), ultimately one term is valued as having positive attributes and the other as having negative attributes. No one really wants a negative label, and in fact, broad categories do not reflect reality, as each one of us is far more complex than any label could express. For example, I was leading a workshop on UDL once and overheard a participant say, "I want to do this for my executive function students." How misguided! In actuality, all learners use the portions of their brains that involve executive functioning, and each learner has both learning needs and strengths in that area. The UDL Guidelines offer you a way to design lessons without categorizing learners.

WHAT IS LEARNING?

The brain is a dense, interconnected set of large and small networks of neurons that communicate with one another along multiple pathways formed as people learn. In applying UDL to lesson planning, it's important to understand how the framework helps to address the act of learning. Simply put, learning is the process of acquiring knowledge and skills as we interact with the world around us.

According to Meyer and colleagues (2014), learning is based on a response to one's environment. In effect, humans learn every time they experience anything. It is integral to the complex context of our experiences. Therefore, your lesson plans should offer your students *experiences.*

> Tell me and I forget. Teach me and I remember. Involve me and I learn.
>
> —Benjamin Franklin

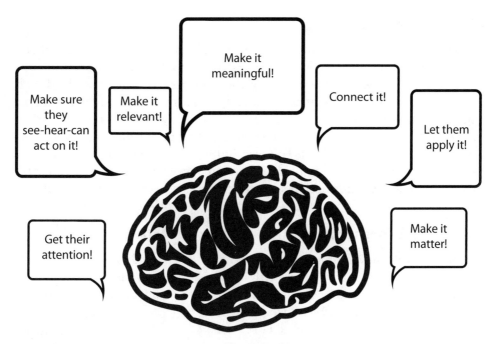

Figure 3.2. The neuroscience of teaching methods.

They should guide students to engage in the learning context or environment and build deep understanding during the process of learning.

In addition, lessons should focus on broader concepts. Some educators focus their lesson designs on providing their students with facts and details to remember rather than larger concepts, such as the cause-and-effect themes evident in an event or illustrated in a text. Nowadays, facts and details are often at our fingertips via web searches on cell phones or computers. How many times have you been in a conversation with a family member or colleague who decides to check on a fact by doing a quick Google or Internet search? The adult learners in my workshops and college classes often have their laptops, tablets, or cell phones handy and will readily see where they can find more details on a topic I mention. It may be an annoying experience for a teacher (especially if students correct you), but it is a fact of life in today's information age. With this in mind, lesson plans should focus on building knowledge of a different kind—a deep understanding that can be transferred and generalized to other contexts (Bransford, Brown, & Cocking, 2000).

THE NEUROSCIENCE OF LESSON PLANNING

Neuroscience research tells us that learning new information involves a multistep process. As you design your lessons, it's helpful to understand the journey that new content traverses as any human being learns—in other words, how the brain builds deep understanding. Using the language of the UDL Guidelines (noted in italics), let's explore how information is processed by our brains in this next section.

Recruiting Interest

When novel information is available, our brains notice it and recognize that it requires attention. Consequently, the first thing that educators need to do in their lessons is to *recruit the interest* of their learners (engagement). By design, the human brain tends to ignore or quickly forget most stimuli in its environment, because there is so much. As a matter of fact, you have 18 to 30 seconds to catch the attention of your learners before their brains dismiss new content (Ebert, Ebert, & Bentley, 2011; Fogarty, 2009). By offering *individual choice* and emphasizing the *relevance and value* of the information, teachers enhance the significance of new information so that learners pay attention to it. What does this mean in terms of your UDL lesson planning? *Get their attention!*

Offering Options for Perception and Physical Action

After discerning novel information, a learner's "short-term memory" holds onto it as the brain decides what to do with it. To ensure that your students are able to alert to and recognize new content, it's critical that you provide *options for perception* (representation), which include *auditory and visual alternatives*. You also need to consider how your learners will initially act on any novel content and provide *options for physical action* as needed (action and expression). What does this mean in terms of your UDL lesson planning? *Make sure they can see it, hear it, and act on it!*

> Anything that is worth teaching can be presented in many different ways.
>
> —Howard Gardner,
> Harvard professor

Sustaining Effort

Once the brain decides that new information is worthy of its attention, its so-called working memory takes over. Research has shown that children can hold information in their working memory for about 5 to 10 minutes and adults can hold it for about 10 to 20 minutes. After that, the information naturally decays or moves to and is stored in long-term memory. While there are individual differences, working memories quickly overload. For example, learners only hold approximately five to seven separate or unrelated bits of information concurrently in working memory (Ebert et al., 2011; Fogarty, 2009; Sousa, 2011).

Working-memory overload impacts your learner's ability to *sustain effort and persist* during your lesson (engagement). By *heightening the salience of your learning goals*—that is, linking them to experiences that are relevant to your learners—you can decrease the impact of working-memory overload. You can also vary or *balance the demands and resources* within your lesson by offering scaffolds and chunking new material into memorable pieces of information. Mnemonics—such as clever words, phrases, lists, steps, acronyms, and rhymes—are a successful device to help learners remember larger amounts of content. For example, the mnemonic phrase "Every good boy does fine" has helped countless music students learn the letter names of the treble staff: E-G-B-D-F. What does this mean in terms of your UDL lesson planning? *Make it relevant!*

Offering Options to Build Understanding

How you present content makes a difference. Neuroscience research indicates that learners remember about 10% of orally presented new information; however, if you present the same information orally with a strong nonlinguistic (i.e., visual or sensory) image, learners recall about 65% (Ebert et al., 2011). While you present new material, you need to focus on helping your learners to assign meaning to the novel content by *providing options for building understanding of the language or mathematical expressions and/or symbols* you're using (representation). You can do that effectively by providing options that *clarify vocabulary and symbols, clarify syntax and structures,* and help learners with *decoding of text, mathematical notations, or other symbols.* You can also make the information more memorable by *illustrating concepts using multimedia,* such as video, slides, graphic organizers, and paired auditory and visual images. If you're working with students who are English language learners or you're teaching a world language, it's critical to also *support understanding across languages* through translations and graphic illustrations (representation). What does this mean in terms of your UDL lesson planning? *Make it meaningful!*

Constructing Deep Understanding

Moving new content from working memory to long-term memory requires educators to *provide options that support comprehension* (representation). Instead of the old idea of students' brains being empty vessels for teachers to fill with knowledge, educators need to help learners construct deep understanding. Neuroscience research confirms that storage in long-term memory involves creating neural pathways of linked stimuli—associated vocabulary, physical sensations, emotional impressions, and perceptions of the environment (Meyer et al., 2014). This is why smelling cinnamon conjures up a vision of your grandmother's breakfast rolls and hearing a song popular when you were a teenager transports you back to the same feelings you had as you entered a high school dance. To build lasting understanding, start with linking novel information with what the learner already knows by *activating background knowledge.* In addition, carefully *highlighting patterns, critical features, big ideas, and relationships* will *guide information processing* (representation) and encourage the development of new neural pathways. What does this mean in terms of your UDL lesson planning? *Connect it!*

Offering Options for Expression and Communication

A successful strategy for promoting movement of new content from working memory to long-term memory is providing learners with multiple experiences with the novel material. Valuable experiences—including opportunities for repetition, rehearsal, and practice—and options for *visualization and manipulation* (representation) build the strong associations needed for creating neural pathways. In particular, expressing what they know to others helps learners link the new information to meaningful situations. You can enhance this meaning-making by *providing options for expression and communication* that include *multimedia, various expressive tools,* and *opportunities for practice and performance.* Furthermore, including *options for employing executive functions* (action and expression) and problem-solving activities, such as case studies that ask learners to apply content to real-life situations, can increase student engagement and, as a result, improve the likelihood that learners will remember new information. Sharing with others through *collaboration* and learner-to-learner discussions also heightens understanding (engagement). What does this mean in terms of your UDL lesson planning? *Let them apply it!*

Promoting Self-Directed Learning

According to researchers, connecting new learning to something that is personally relevant enhances moving novel information to long-term memory (Fogarty, 2009). *Guiding appropriate goal setting* by asking learners to define personal learning goals is important not only at the beginning of your lesson but also at the point when you want students to assign meaning. As a matter of fact, self-directed learners know how they learn. They take advantage of effective *mastery-oriented feedback* (engagement) and *support for planning and strategy development* to *monitor their own progress* (action and expression). Additionally, educators who provide *options for self-regulation*—such as *promoting high expectations, coping strategies, and self-assessment and reflection techniques* (engagement)—help students to focus their efforts on building deep understanding. What does this mean in terms of your UDL lesson planning? *Make it matter!*

In summary, the neuroscience of learning guides effective lessons. With this knowledge, you can design successful UDL lessons by remembering these seven actions

1. Get their attention

2. Make sure they can see it, hear it, and act on it

3. Make it relevant

4. Make it meaningful

5. Connect it

6. Let them apply it

7. Make it matter

WHAT IS LEARNER VARIABILITY?

There are several excellent resources that illustrate the brain research undergirding each of the UDL Guidelines, so this book will not duplicate that information (see Meyer et al., 2014; Nelson, 2014). You are already familiar with at least an introductory description of how the three large brain networks align with the UDL Guidelines from Chapter 1; however, it's valuable to understand the role of these brain networks and learner variability in order to effectively attend to them in your UDL lesson planning. Figure 3.3 illustrates the function of the three brain networks as defined by UDL.

Universal Design for Learning

Affective networks:
THE WHY OF LEARNING

Recognition networks:
THE WHAT OF LEARNING

Strategic networks:
THE HOW OF LEARNING

How learners get engaged and stay motivated. How they are challenged, excited, or interested. These are affective dimensions.

How we gather facts and categorize what we see, hear, and read. Identifying letters, words, or an author's style are recognition tasks.

Planning and performing tasks. How we organize and express our ideas. Writing an essay or solving a math problem are strategic tasks.

Stimulate interest and motivation for learning

Present information and content in different ways

Differentiate the ways that students can express what they know

Figure 3.3. Three networks = three UDL principles. (From © CAST, 2012. Used with permission. All rights reserved.)

Experienced educators like Brian know that individual learners are unique and that they learn in ways that vary. In fact, neuroscience research demonstrates how unique each human being is. Each individual brain has a distinct pattern of activity. Even identical twins are dissimilar in some ways. Although individuals are different, there is a systematic organization to how humans learn. What is especially helpful to educators is that the UDL Guidelines illustrate the variable characteristics found in any group of people. So even if you don't know the specific strengths or needs of every learner, you can anticipate and design for learner variability in your lesson plans (Meyer et al., 2014).

Some educators believe they need to know each learner first before they can effectively design lessons that take all learners' needs into account. They wait until they've developed learner profiles for their students to plan substantial lessons. Other educators have so many students in their classes—perhaps more than a hundred—that addressing the individual learning needs of each student appears to be a pipedream. The advantage of applying the UDL Guidelines in your lesson planning is that they offer systematic, predictable characteristics of variability that allow you to proactively meet all learners' needs. In essence, using the UDL framework offers educators a broader view, a dynamic collage of strengths, needs, interests, preferences, and dispositions—a variability perspective.

> The only constant is variability.
> —Josh Zimmerman,
> CTE Teacher Specialist,
> Maryland

THREE LARGE NETWORKS WORK TOGETHER TO LEARN

The UDL Guidelines are structured to represent how people vary in their learning. Let's explore how the guidelines align with lesson planning.

Affective Networks and Engagement

The affective networks, located in the center of the brain, monitor the environment to set priorities, motivate and engage learners, and monitor their behavior. Affective networks help learners initiate actions and respond based on how they feel about what they perceive. According to Meyer and colleagues, "Emotion organizes, drives, amplifies, and attenuates students' thinking and reasoning" (2014, p. 12).

For example, Brian's students appear to be nervous and struggling when he calls on them to answer questions in class. Does this tell us that they perceive his learning environment as threatening? Or, bored by his lecture, have they given in to classroom distractions and not actually heard the question? In either case, Brian

> I've learned that people will forget what you said, people will forget what you did, but people will never forget how you made them feel.
>
> —Maya Angelou

needs to use engagement strategies that will positively activate his students' affective networks. Figure 3.4 illustrates guidelines for engagement.

Figure 3.4. Engagement guidelines. (From © CAST, 2012. Used with permission. All rights reserved.)

Think about your own engagement strengths and preferences for a moment, and consider the following scenarios:

- How anxious do you feel before you take a test? Do you think your anxiety affects your performance?

- Visualize that you're working with your family to organize a weeklong family vacation and one family member keeps interrupting you or repeating what you're saying. Does this environment cause you to lose focus or feel stressed?

- How productive are the meetings you attend? Are they aimless, meandering to unclear conclusions, or are they purposeful and relevant? Are there unresolved personal conflicts? In any case, think about how you feel just prior to joining the meeting. How do you prepare emotionally? How do previous experiences affect your performance during meetings?

Exercise Your Affective Networks   What motivates you? This short motivation quiz may reveal how you engage in a learning environment and offer insights on ways to engage your learners. Ask a colleague, friend, or your PLC members to take the quiz as featured in Figure 3.5, and then compare your answers. How much variability is there?

Choose Engagement Strategies   As you look at the learning goals—but before you add assessments, methods, materials, and media to your lesson plan—consider whether you'll need to:

Recruit interest

- Provide choice and options for learner autonomy

- Heighten the lesson's relevance, value, and authenticity for learners

- Minimize threats and distractions within the environment

Sustain effort and persistence

- Raise the importance of the lesson's goal

- Evaluate the balance between the demands of the goal and the resources available for learners to achieve it

- Build in opportunities for collaboration with peers

Provide options for self-regulation

- Create mastery-oriented steps toward accomplishment of the goal

- Promote higher expectations for success

- Eliminate potentially frustrating or stressful circumstances

- Provide for learner self-assessment

Motivation Quiz—What Motivates You?

Questions	Response
1. I prefer to choose goals and objectives that are personally valuable to me.	❏ Not at all ❏ Sometimes ❏ Often ❏ Very often
2. I'm sure of my ability to achieve my goals.	❏ Not at all ❏ Sometimes ❏ Often ❏ Very often
3. When working on my goals, I put in maximum effort.	❏ Not at all ❏ Sometimes ❏ Often ❏ Very often
4. I use rewards (and consequences) to keep myself focused.	❏ Not at all ❏ Sometimes ❏ Often ❏ Very often
5. I never worry about deadlines and getting things done on time.	❏ Not at all ❏ Sometimes ❏ Often ❏ Very often
6. I regularly check on my progress and use that information to adjust my efforts.	❏ Not at all ❏ Sometimes ❏ Often ❏ Very often
7. When an unexpected event threatens or distracts me from my goal, I stick with it anyway.	❏ Not at all ❏ Sometimes ❏ Often ❏ Very often
8. Sharing my goals with family, friends, or colleagues helps me to stay motivated.	❏ Not at all ❏ Sometimes ❏ Often ❏ Very often
9. I create a vivid and powerful vision of success before embarking work on a goal.	❏ Not at all ❏ Sometimes ❏ Often ❏ Very often

Figure 3.5. Motivation Quiz—What Motivates You?

Case Example 1: Applying the UDL Principle of Engagement

A high school English teacher, Sarah is using poetry to teach how themes develop in text. She's developed the following learning goal: Students will analyze how Long-fellow's poem "Paul Revere's Ride" uses descriptive words and phrases to create a theme of urgency and speed in Revere's ride and express their conclusions using a choice of media (e.g., slides, video, paper) in a short (3-minute) presentation at a proficient or higher level, as measured by a presentation rubric. (See Table 4.2 for a rubric example.)

Sarah's learning goal is a SMART goal that offers flexibility and choice. However, as she considers the learner variability in her class, she antici-pates students who are not familiar with the descriptive words, such as the English language learners, will need access to an online dictionary that offers translations. Allowing dictionary access will *minimize student anxiety* and *balance the goal demands and needed resources*. She also realizes that the urgency of a horse gallop may not be relevant for those students who have never seen or been on a horse. To *recruit interest*, Sarah decides to begin the lesson with a brief brainstorming session in order to *heighten authenticity* and to allow students to share what they already know about how fast horses can go. Finally, knowing that some of her students lack *self-regulation skills* and need guidance to create the presentation, she opts to share the product rubric as part of the lesson introduction and to allow students to *work collaboratively* in pairs on the presentations.

Recognition Networks and Representation

The recognition networks, located toward the back of the brain, sense and per-ceive information in the environment and transform it into usable knowledge. Meyer and colleagues assert that recognition networks "differ in hundreds of thousands of ways" (2014, p. 68) because they are created over time in response to our individual experiences. Learners are constantly taking in information and building understanding based on the complex context of the learning situ-ation. New perceptions are therefore biased by what individuals already know. Figure 3.6 illustrates guidelines for representation.

Now consider your own representation strengths and preferences:

- Would you prefer to read a book, listen to an audio version of the story, or watch the movie? Does it matter to you if you see a movie before you read the book? Some people have strong opinions about this.

- Do you think you get more from data displayed in a list or Excel file or in a graph or pie chart?

- Think about a time when you were trying to communicate with someone who spoke a different language. How much did you rely on gestures, facial expres-sions, and the person's tone of voice to understand what he or she was saying?

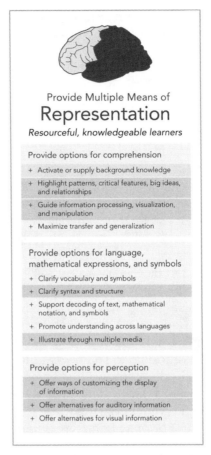

Figure 3.6. Representation guidelines. (From © CAST, 2012. Used with permission. All rights reserved.)

- How frustrating is it for you to listen to someone whose hands are in front of his or her mouth when talking? How much do you need that visual information?

- Have you ever tried to watch a movie when the audio is slightly out of sync with the video? How difficult is that for you? At one time or another, most of us have experienced a curious illusion known as the McGurk effect, a perceptual phenomenon that occurs when auditory and visual information do not match. When the sound you hear visually appears to be a different sound from that being said, you perceive a third sound.

 **Learning Link**

Curious to learn more about the McGurk effect? Watch this video by the BBC at https://www.youtube.com/watch?v=G-lN8vWm3m0.

The Myth of Teaching to Perceptual Learning Styles You may know that research has discredited the idea that people possess specific learning styles (e.g., so-called auditory learners or visual learners) and that instruction aimed at those perceptual learning styles does not produce better results (Pashler, McDaniel, Rohrer, & Bjork, 2008). How you perceive information is mostly dependent on _context_. For instance, in one situation you may rely on your auditory skills, and in another you may find your visual perceptual or tactile skills take the lead. Nonetheless, learners readily identify what they think is their learning preference given a certain context. The key is to provide multiple options for perception in your lessons without rigidly limiting who has access. Your learners may very well surprise you!

Exercise Your Recognition Networks How strong are your English comprehension skills, especially for word recognition? Try to unscramble the words in Figure 3.7 and, while you do it, analyze what characteristics help you to be successful.

How easy is this for you? Ask a colleague, family member, or friend to complete the task. How much variability is there between your skills and others? Is it easier if you know the context—that all these words come from the representation column in the UDL Guidelines? Does it help to know that the first and last letters are in the correct places and only the letters in the middle of each word are scrambled?

Determine Representation Strategies As you did earlier, look at your learning goals—and before you add assessments, methods, materials, and media to your lesson plan—determine whether you'll need to

Provide options for perception

- Customize how information is displayed

- Offer alternatives for auditory information

- Offer alternatives for visual information

Provide scaffolding for understanding text, mathematical notation, and symbols

- Clarify vocabulary or symbols

- Clarify syntax and structure

Provide scaffolding for decoding of text, mathematical notation, and symbols

Provide translations to promote understanding across languages

- Illustrate information using multiple media

Promote comprehension skills

- Activate or supply background knowledge

- Highlight patterns, critical features, big ideas, and relationships

Provide scaffolding for transfer and generalization

- Offer guidance for information processing, visualization, and manipulation

REPRESENTATION SCRAMBLE PUZZLE

Please unscramble the words below.

1. Cinosomerpehn _____

2. Pcteopiern _____

3. Ilalusrtte _____

4. Claifry _____

5. Daslipy _____

6. Tserafnr _____

7. Vaaolrcbuy _____

8. Eiexorsspns _____

9. Oitpons _____

10. Sblyoms _____

Figure 3.7. Representation Scramble Puzzle. (Answers are on the last page of this chapter.)

Case Example 2: Applying the UDL Principle of Representation

Mario decides to start his UDL implementation journey by first applying the UDL Principle of Representation in lesson planning for his Western Civilization course. He develops a flexible, SMART goal to guide his thinking: Students will analyze and synthesize multiple media sources to produce a comparative analysis of the revolution motivators for the French and American revolutions at a competent to proficient level (as measured by a product rubric). As Mario views his learning goal and anticipates the learner variability in his class, he decides he needs to concentrate on offering varying displays of the information. Instead of relying on just the text, he will offer the students a list of articles accessible online and some videos that share accurate accounts of the French culture prior to the revolution. He also realizes that he could *represent and clarify vocabulary* and the prevalent thoughts, concepts, and language of each culture by starting his class with a brainstorming exercise using a graphic organizer drawn on the whiteboard and available in printed form if students prefer. He will write, *What were the causes of the French and American revolutions?* in the middle of a circle, and then he will *activate students' background knowledge* information by asking them to add branches for their ideas, such as *high taxes*. He realizes he could *explain French language concepts* as students add them to the graphic organizer. He will then make copies of the final product available on the course wiki so that students can *apply the big ideas* in creating their comparison analyses.

Strategic Networks and Action and Expression

The strategic networks (located in the front of the brain) plan, organize, initiate, sequence, coordinate, and monitor purposeful actions in the environment. This part of the brain—the cortex—controls a continuum of motor movements, from simple actions, such as turning the pages of a book, to more complex actions, such as speaking, dancing, playing an instrument (e.g., piano, violin), or playing a sport (e.g., hockey, gymnastics). With practice, motor actions can become routinized so that they require less conscious effort (Meyer et al., 2014).

The UDL Guidelines for the Principle of Action and Expression also include strategies related to strategic planning, called *executive function skills*. Figure 3.8 illustrates guidelines for action and expression. These are complex cognitive strategies, such as identifying goals, organizing and making a plan, executing a plan, self-monitoring, and correcting actions. If they sound a bit like the steps to lesson planning to you, they are. Lesson planning requires a high level of organization and strategic thinking and is a great example of how you use your brain's executive functions.

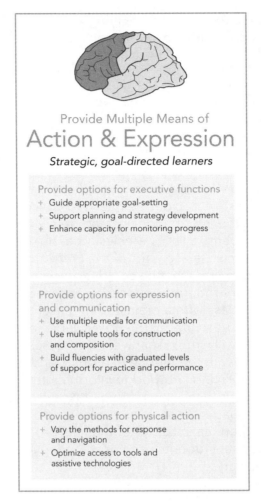

Provide Multiple Means of
Action & Expression
Strategic, goal-directed learners

Provide options for executive functions
+ Guide appropriate goal-setting
+ Support planning and strategy development
+ Enhance capacity for monitoring progress

Provide options for expression
and communication
+ Use multiple media for communication
+ Use multiple tools for construction
  and composition
+ Build fluencies with graduated levels
  of support for practice and performance

Provide options for physical action
+ Vary the methods for response
  and navigation
+ Optimize access to tools and
  assistive technologies

Figure 3.8. Action and Expression Guidelines. (From © CAST, 2012. Used with permission. All rights reserved.)

Take a few minutes to reflect on your own action and expression strengths and preferences:

- Would you prefer to write with a pen or pencil or use a digital tool to keep track of your calendar? Some people have access to digital tools and know how to use them but need to physically note events on a paper calendar.

- Do you readily use a variety of apps for various personal or professional tasks, or is this still unchartered territory for you?

- Think about a time when you were at a planning meeting. Were you able to cut through all the verbiage to find the core goal or next step, whereas others seemed confused, or did you wait for someone else to articulate the goal or planning step and then jump in to refine it? Goal setting requires synthesis skills, which are easy for some but a chore for others.

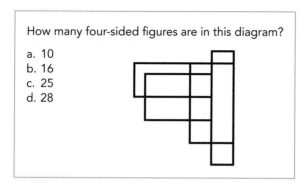

How many four-sided figures are in this diagram?

a. 10
b. 16
c. 25
d. 28

Figure 3.9. Learner Variability Exercise A. (Answer is on the last page of this chapter.)

Exercise Your Strategic Networks   What types of puzzles do you prefer? Select one of the following puzzles in Figures 3.9, 3.10, and 3.11. Ask others to solve the same puzzle, and while you problem solve, take note of the strategies you use. Discuss the strategies you used. How much variability is there?

Case Example 3: Applying the Principle of Action and Expression

Cindy wants to be sure her second-graders understand how to use addition with even numbers. She's developed the following flexible, SMART goal: *Students will determine whether a group of objects (up to 20) has an even number of members, devise an equation to express the even number as a sum of two equal addends, and show their answers using a provided worksheet or digital format with 80% accuracy.* Before she writes her lesson plan, she takes a look at her goal and the guidelines under the UDL Principle of Action and Expression. She asks, "What options for action and expression will be most helpful in addressing the learner variability of her students?" Most of her learners can write numerals to 20, but two of the children have difficulty with handwriting, making their written products almost illegible.

Which animal out of the five listed below is most unlike the others?

a. Tiger
b. Dog
c. Snake
d. Fox
e. Bear

Figure 3.10. Learner Variability Exercise B. (Answers are on the last page of this chapter.)

Which one of the four letter designs below is
least like the other three?

H   M   E   W

Figure 3.11.   Learner Variability Exercise C. (Answers are on the last
page of this chapter.)

Giving students the option of completing the worksheet using one of the
class computer tablets (*use of media*) will offer a *viable choice in how they
respond*. One student with a significant physical disability needs to have
access to assistive technology, his augmentative communication device,
to express himself, because he can't write with a pencil. Cindy realizes that
some students will need manipulatives to *support their planning*. She'll
also create equation strips (i.e., students match items to each side of the
equation) as optional scaffolds for those who want to use them. To *build
greater fluency* and independence, she'll arrange for students to work in
small groups to develop equations for the first two groups of items and
then complete the rest of the equations by themselves.

Consider Action and Expression Strategies   Again, take a look at the
learning goals before adding other elements to your lesson plan, such as the
assessments, methods, or materials, and consider whether you need to:

Provide options for physical action

- Vary how learners can respond and navigate the environment
- Optimize access to tools and assistive technology

Provide options for expression and communication

- Use and encourage use of multiple media for communication
- Use and encourage use of multiple media for construction and purpose
- Build fluency of responses with graduated levels of support for practice
  and performance

Promote executive function skills

- Offer guidance for appropriate goal setting
- Support planning and strategy development

Facilitate ways to manage information and resources

- Build and enhance progress monitoring skills

EXPERT LEARNERS

Your ultimate goal for applying UDL to your practice may be to enhance your
craft as an educator, to improve your students' test scores, or to target some

other idea. CAST researchers suggest that the goal of applying UDL to instruction is to guide students to become expert learners (Meyer et al., 2014). *Expert learners* are purposeful, motivated, resourceful, knowledgeable, strategic, and goal directed. The key aspect of developing expert learners is that anyone can become one. The description is not related to how well a learner does on tests, how many degrees he or she has, or how quickly he or she can solve puzzles. These are characteristics everyone can strive to achieve. Chapter 8 delves into expert learning in more depth.

SUMMARY

How educators view learners impacts their students' learning. Understanding how your students learn and how variable your learners are will maximize your instruction. Learning is more than knowing facts and details; it is the *process of gaining knowledge or skills by studying, practicing, being taught, or experiencing* our environment. The UDL framework helps educators support this learning process effectively. Neuroscience tells us that new information is processed by the brain in a specific manner. First, a learner alerts to novel content using his or her short-term memory. Then working memory holds onto it until it's deemed worthy of remembering. Finally, the content moves into long-term memory or is dismissed. Providing your students with *experiences* in your lessons will move new information into long-term memory and help them to build a deep understanding that is transferable to other contexts. Seven actions you can take in your lessons to help learners move novel content to long-term memory are

1. Get their attention

2. Make sure they can see it, hear it, and act on it

3. Make it relevant

4. Make it meaningful

5. Connect it

6. Let them apply it

7. Make it matter

Even though each individual brain has a distinct pattern of activity, the UDL Guidelines offer systematic, predictable characteristics of variability that you can use to design your lessons. To effectively plan for learner variability, it's important to understand the roles of the three key brain networks in learning:

1. Affective networks help learners initiate actions and respond based on how they feel about what they perceive.

2. Recognition networks control how learners perceive information, which is greatly influenced by context.

3. Strategic networks plan, organize, initiate, sequence, coordinate, and monitor purposeful actions.

In essence, the UDL framework offers educators a dynamic collage of learner strengths, needs, interests, preferences, and dispositions—a *variability perspective*.

LEARNER VARIABILITY EXERCISE ANSWERS

Representation Scramble Puzzle answers: 1) Comprehension, 2) Perception, 3) Illustrate, 4) Clarify, 5) Display, 6) Transfer, 7) Vocabulary, 8) Expressions, 9) Options, 10) Symbols.

Exercise A answer: d) 28.

Exercise B answer: c) Snake. (It has no legs.)

Exercise C answer: H. (It can be made with three lines and the others are made with four lines.)

UDL LESSON PLANNING IN ACTION

To add to your understanding of learner variability, you may want to view a video (approximately 3 minutes in length) that illustrates the second step in the UDL lesson planning process, taking a variability perspective. (See Video 3.1: Taking a Variability Perspective [go online to see the video].) You'll meet Brian, a college professor who is changing how he designs his courses by applying the UDL lesson planning process. He realizes that students learn in a variety of ways and that their individual strengths, needs, interests, and experiences are different. Brian also knows that all learners use a multistep process to learn new information.

Watch this video to see how educators 1) recruit their learners' attention; 2) customize how information is displayed; 3) design opportunities for collaboration; 4) clarify and scaffold understanding of text, symbols, vocabulary, and sentences by using physical actions and multimedia; 5) highlight patterns, critical features, big ideas, and relationships; 6) offer choice and access to tools, media, and multiple options for expression; and 7) promote goal setting and self-assessment.

4

Assessing Learning

Making It Matter

This chapter discusses various aspects of formative and summative assessments, how to incorporate meaningful measurement in lesson planning based on UDL, and how to develop classroom-based assessments to guide instruction, such as rubrics.

What am I looking for? Chandra asks herself after poring over a set of quizzes from her 24 fourth-graders. Her class just finished a unit on Colonial times, and this quiz was the final assessment. Chandra applies the UDL Guidelines to her instruction but not to her assessment strategies. It never seemed necessary. Each year her class does a couple of engaging projects, which she evaluates with a rubric. But ordinarily, to check on student understanding, Chandra relies on short multiple-choice quizzes. "A quiz is tried and true, quick and easy," she says. Yet so many of her students didn't answer the questions correctly on the Colonial times unit quiz that she now wonders if a quiz was the best way to assess their learning. On the basis of the test results, she still doesn't know what they've learned or if they met the unit learning goal. Chandra continues her lamenting: Maybe I should have had them write an essay? Would that have given me better information? What evidence do I need anyway? What should I be measuring? What student performance really matters?

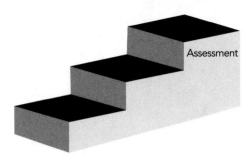

Chandra is a good teacher who's stuck. She doesn't know enough about the assessment process to determine what her students are learning; and, although she's familiar with UDL, she doesn't understand how to use the UDL framework to select or develop measures that match her instruction. Chandra's lesson planning process looks like this: She develops flexible, SMART goals; considers learner variability for her instructional design; plans the lesson content; and then chooses an assessment from her limited list of tried-and-true options. She not only skips the crucial step of considering the UDL framework for assessment selection but also thoughtlessly tags evaluation of student learning onto the end of her process. Although her SMART learning goal is measureable, she's not measuring her instruction in a meaningful way. As a result, Chandra is not as informed about her students' learning as she could be.

Effective teachers do more than merely give tests; they understand that the right assessment matched to the learning goal and complemented by UDL strategies can increase the success of their lessons. The third step in the UDL lesson planning process is matching your clearly defined learning goal with a *flexible, meaningful* assessment. To make sure that your instruction is making a difference—that it matters—you need to know the basics of how to best measure student learning.

> The measure of who we are is what we do with what we have.
> —Vince Lombardi

This chapter applies the UDL principles to understanding the *why, what,* and *how* of assessments. In addition to outlining typical reasons for doing assessments and highlighting the characteristics of effective assessments aligned with UDL, this chapter recommends five fundamental questions to address when deciding your lesson's assessment; clarifies the difference between summative and formative assessments; offers examples of classroom assessments; and explains how to create flexible, informative assessments, such as rubrics. Let's get started!

WHY GIVE ASSESSMENTS?

Chandra uses quizzes to determine grades. Similarly, most educators use assessments primarily for two reasons: 1) to evaluate students' progress along a continuum of learning targets and 2) to plan instructional improvement. Other reasons for conducting assessment may come to mind as well. Some are within your control, and some are not.

 Take Note

Rudner and Schafer (2002) offer additional reasons for conducting assessments: 1) to establish student "baseline" or readiness levels, particularly at the beginning of the school year, class, or course; 2) to determine grouping; 3) to help determine pacing of content delivery; 4) to make decisions about promotion and retention; and 5) for sharing information with stakeholders.

Accountability

The word *assessment* usually conjures up images of students sitting in rows and taking mandated standardized tests. Although standardized testing is only one piece of the assessment picture, it hovers over most of us because of its high-stakes accountability impact. The state and other authorities use standardized tests to determine if schools or districts measure up to a predetermined bar of proficiency. Plus, student standardized test results recently began to play a role in teacher evaluation systems in many places in the United States and are now a factor in whether educators receive bonuses or stay employed. Although there is a current effort to develop standardized tests aligned with the UDL principles, the vast majority of standardized tests used for accountability purposes are not flexible enough to be useful for UDL lesson planning. I will discuss this at greater depth later in this chapter.

Diagnostic Evaluation

Some educators administer tests and interpret the results for the purpose of diagnosing student readiness, strengths, weaknesses, and levels of performance compared to a statistical norm. For college assessors, special educators, English as a second language teachers, and specialized instructional-support personnel (e.g., school psychologists, speech-language pathologists, occupational therapists), administering diagnostic assessments is a major part of their professional responsibilities. The purpose of these evaluations is to determine student placement in remedial, supplemental, or advanced courses or student eligibility for special services, such as programs for English language learners, students with gifts/talents, and students with disabilities. Again, typical diagnostic evaluations are standardized assessments and are not useful for UDL lesson planning.

Assessment of Learning

I've heard some educators say, "If I didn't have to give tests, I wouldn't." I know I used to say it. Today you probably give assignments because, like Chandra, you need some data or evidence for grading your learners' progress. *Assessments of learning* are part of the instruction process, are formative in nature, and serve as a map or GPS for both educators and learners in charting the right course toward mastery of the learning goal, keeping everyone on the road toward achievement. They support UDL implementation well because they are flexible and still provide teachers with evidence of student learning. Not only do they document the ability of learners to answer questions; they also provide information about how learners reason and problem solve. Meaningful assessments, aligned with the UDL principles and matched to your learning goal, can point to what your students have learned and how effective your instruction has been.

 **Reflection**

Do you believe the following statements about assessment are true or false? How do they correspond to your thinking?

- Assessment of learning is formative. It occurs during classroom tasks and lessons and can be an informal check-in to determine where students are in the general pacing of a lesson.

- Assessment of learning is summative. It determines a level of student performance at a specific point in time.

Assessment for Learning

Effective assessments provide both educators and students with information regarding how well learning goals have been achieved and what students need to learn next. In a student-centered UDL learning environment, formative assessment is an integral part of instruction, teaching learners how they learn and how to regulate their own learning. For instance, by using various strategies, such as folders, portfolios, or information management systems, learners are involved in keeping track of their own learning.

WHAT IS ASSESSMENT?

Chandra has a limited view of assessment. It is far more comprehensive than simply giving a quiz or standardized test. Assessment is the process of gathering and interpreting information or data about learner performance in order to measure or judge that performance (Marzano, 2010). If your assessments align with the UDL framework, they are flexible, ongoing, informative, and meaningful. They measure both product and process and actively inform and involve learners (Meyer et al., 2014). Since no one assessment is perfect, it is crucial to use multiple ways to gather evidence of what students have learned.

 **Take Note**

Keep in mind that any assessment is a snapshot of performance at a specific time and within a certain context, and it is likely to have errors. Consequently, never use one single test by itself to make an important decision for anyone (Rudner & Schaeffer, 2002; Suskie, 2009).

Assessments fall into two categories: formative and summative. In brief, *formative assessments* are defined as ongoing measurements that guide instruction. In contrast, *summative assessments*, such as the quizzes that Chandra administers, are usually conducted for the purpose of grading or making a final judgment about performance, because they measure student learning after instruction is complete. I will explain these two types of assessments in more detail later in this chapter.

HOW TO MAKE UDL LESSONS MATTER

To make your lessons matter, start by examining your learning goal. Frankly, if you've written a SMART goal, you've already considered how to make it measurable. Your lesson assessment should 1) align with your learning goal, 2) measure the attainment of specific skills or knowledge content, and 3) offer you information you can use to judge the success of your instructional techniques. To identify what evidence of student learning you need, consider these six characteristics and corresponding questions:

> Our lives begin to end the day we become silent about things that matter.
> —Martin Luther King, Jr.

1. *Alignment*—How will you align your assessment with your learning goal? What are the key knowledge, skills, or dispositions that you want students to demonstrate?

2. *Quality*—What attributes or characteristics are you expecting to see? What do you feel represents quality work?

3. *Performance level*—How can you define skill development from novice to expert for expertise that exists along a continuum? What performance level of work are you expecting? Are you going to allow for drafts and revisions?

4. *Expression*—How do you expect learners to submit their work? As a performance, presentation, or exhibit? As part of a group project? Electronically? What choices of media will you permit? Will you allow assignments to be resubmitted?

5. *Reflection*—How will you know which parts of your instruction were effective or ineffective?

6. *Feedback*—How will you share your evaluation with learners? How will you respond if students don't meet the learning goal?

Optimize Success

To help your learners be successful, you need to provide clear instructions for completing the assessment in multiple ways (e.g., written with key aspects highlighted, verbal, graphic organizer). Don't assume your learners will know what you expect. UDL expert Dr. Peggy Coyne talks about the "Guess what's on my mind" phenomenon: Educators know what they want but neglect to share that expectation clearly with learners. As a result, students are forced to make an uninformed assumption, and their teachers are inevitably disappointed with their assignments. Be explicit, especially if this assignment is different from ones you've used before. Rubrics and checklists are valuable ways to guide assignment completion. Or you can offer a model or example of what constitutes quality work.

To accurately measure progress, scrutinize assessment results to identify any misunderstandings or misconceptions you may need to address during that class session or in future ones. Look for patterns in your evidence demonstrating that learners are synthesizing the learning into a whole that can be transferred and generalized to other tasks or concepts. Reteaching often involves simply doing the same thing, just more slowly. Instead, consider *corrective instruction,* which highlights the errors or mistakes at the beginning of new instruction (Stiggins, 1998). For example, at the end of his social studies class, Sean often uses exit ticket summaries he calls the "dozen words of less" ticket. Each student is expected to state one fact they learned in a one-sentence assessment of 12 words or less. To keep it interesting and offer choice, he varies how students submit their assessments (e.g., oral statements, sticky notes on a wall chart, written exit tickets, backchannel responses). He's able to quickly scan the summaries for evidence that the class understood the lesson's big ideas. If there are any misunderstandings, he can address them as he plans for his next class.

> We all need people who will give us feedback. That's how we improve.
>
> —Bill Gates

Give Feedback to Learners

Provide clear, meaningful feedback to your learners. Instructive feedback is prompt, ongoing, goal referenced, understandable, and actionable (Wiggins, 2012). Portfolios; project-based learning; self-assessment journals; and data analytics through charts, graphics, or digital displays are excellent examples of assessments that keep learners informed about their current progress and assist with goal-directed learning (i.e., self-regulation). These assessments are measures *for* learning. They reinforce instruction infused with UDL and encourage students to become expert learners. Why? Because assessments that provide meaningful feedback to learners result in students who are wise users of assessment data themselves and who take responsibility for their own learning. Chapter 8 will delve deeper into the concept of learner self-reflection.

Reflection

Do you believe the following statements about assessment are true or false? How do they compare with your thinking?

- Assessment for learning is summative, because it includes a collection of information on student performance gleaned throughout or at a designated time period.

- Assessment for learning allows students to become aware of their own learning strategies and helps them identify their own areas of strengths and needs.

FIVE FUNDAMENTAL QUESTIONS

Chandra feels her assessment selection of multiple-choice quizzes is tried and true—but maybe not. Since she's unsure what her test results indicate about her students' learning, her quiz may not be as *true* as she thinks. If your assessments align with the UDL framework, they will be accurate, appropriate, and meaningful for all your learners. It is your responsibility to ensure the assessments you use do not inadvertently create barriers for your learners. Let's explore that concept further. The following five fundamental questions will help you to select and/or design assessments that align with UDL and take into account key psychometric attributes.

1. Is My Assessment Accessible?

Assessments that are accessible address the mobility and communication needs of learners, particularly students with disabilities who need specialized formats, such as individuals with sensory, physical, or cognitive disabilities. Designing assessments with accessibility in mind from the beginning means all learners perform better and reduces the need for accommodations (Dolan & Hall, 2007). Using the same inaccessible assessment features for everyone isn't fair; in fact, it's inherently unfair. To evaluate the accessibility of your assessments, use the Assessment Accessibility Checklist in Figure 4.1.

Learning Link

To explore resources on accessibility, check out the National Center on Accessible Educational Materials web site at http://aem.cast.org/.

Assessment Accessibility Checklist

DIRECTIONS: The following checklist offers questions for your consideration to ensure that your assessment features meet minimum accessibility criteria.

Accessibility features	Meets criterion
1. Uses consistent, simple, and intuitive format *Is the test taker able to anticipate the format?* Does the assessment maintain consistent format without unnecessary complexity, such as filling buttons or checking boxes, rather than mixing formats? Are the headings and text sizes consistent with the importance of each section?	Yes No
2. Provides options for perception *Is the test taker provided multiple options for visual, auditory, and tactile perception?* Does the text describe images to provide necessary background information? If needed, are images available as tactile graphics for blind test takers? If needed, is auditory information available in a visual form for deaf or hearing impaired test takers? Are specialized formats available? Is the format compatible for use with assistive technology devices or braille? Is written information legible?	Yes No
3. Provides options for flexible physical action *Is the test taker provided options for physical action and expression?* Are alternative response modes available, such as use of an assistive technology device or a human scribe to record answers, if needed? Is the assessment accessible to both right- and left-handed learners?	Yes No
4. Minimizes physical effort *Is the test taker provided with options that require low physical effort?* Does the assessment minimize the need for repetitive actions? Does it offer engagement options without requiring sustained physical effort?	Yes No
5. Minimizes distractions and threats *Is the test taken in a nonthreatening environment? Is the test taker able to screen out unwanted visual and/or auditory distractions?* Is the use of irrelevant pictures, graphics, or formatting features avoided?	Yes No

Your UDL Lesson Planner: The Step-by-Step Guide for Teaching All Learners, by Patti Kelly Ralabate.
Copyright © 2016 by Paul H. Brookes Publishing Co., Inc. All rights reserved.

Figure 4.1.   Assessment Accessibility Checklist.

2. Is My Assessment Flexible?

Assessments in line with the UDL framework are flexible and allow for learner variability. Scaffolds are available for those who need them, and learners have choices in how they express their learning. Using a flexible verb in your learning goal will lead you to consider various, adjustable options for your assessments. Let's return to Chandra's use of multiple-choice quizzes. It's not a flexible assessment; it's rather rigid actually—expecting that all learners will be able to use a paper-and-pencil format and that their responses to the multiple-choice questions will capture adequate evidence of learning. Her assessment would have been more flexible if she had offered her learners the choice of composing a short essay, developing a brief presentation using multiple media options (e.g., slides with audio or a video-captured oral presentation), or creating a poster or graphic display. Using a rubric to evaluate these products would give Chandra the evidence of learning she needs.

3. Is My Assessment Free of Bias?

Bias relates to how *fair* the assessment is and impacts how well it accurately reflects what learners know or are able to do. Popham and Lindheim define potentially biased assessment elements as "anything in an item that could potentially advantage or disadvantage any subgroup of examinees within the populations to be tested" (1980, p. 6). It's easy to see that a science assessment that requires students to write grammatically correct sentences favors native English speakers and adds an unnecessary burden for English language learners. There are other kinds of bias, however. Assessments need to be free of content that would privilege learners with certain experiences or disadvantage those who have little experience with the vocabulary, context, or topic. For instance, students who've never been to a museum would be at a disadvantage if the assessment required

Figure 4.2. Scales of justice.

that they visualize a museum corridor. Additional scaffolding or opportunities to learn about museums would be necessary prior to including this task in an assessment. Another form of unintended bias, offensive in nature, is characterization of individuals by race, gender, ethnicity, disability, religion, or socioeconomic or other backgrounds; you should always avoid this in your assessments.

4. Is My Assessment Valid?

Educators often misunderstand test validity. Generally, assessment validity focuses on how meaningful or relevant the assessment results are. Messick (1996) explains that the content knowledge or skills an assessment reveals must represent the *true* content you are looking to measure. Some researchers refer to designing assessments with *construct relevancy,* meaning that you design them to measure a specific construct—that is, a knowledge, skill, or attribute (Meyer et al., 2014). Let's consider Dave's case: Since he knows word problems can potentially be invalid or not construct relevant if they require reading levels that are problematic for learners with reading difficulties, Dave always checks the reading levels of the language he uses in his math tests. In reality, the task of reading the word problems can muddy his interpretation of the test results, because the assessment ends up measuring both mathematics and reading skills. He could easily misinterpret the test results to mean that his learners didn't know how to apply the mathematical concepts, whereas they actually didn't know how to read the passage. By monitoring reading levels and applying the UDL Guidelines as scaffolds for learners who may have difficulty reading the passages, Dave is able to develop assessments that are meaningful—that are *valid*—assessing what he wants to measure.

5. Is My Assessment Reliable?

Certain things need to be reliable. A fire alarm, for example, needs to work every time it's activated. There is no tolerance for mistakes.

Standardized-test developers go to great lengths to verify that their assessments are reliable (i.e., the assessments contain minimal measurement error). If administered multiple times to the same group under the same conditions, reliable assessments yield very similar results. Statisticians argue that tests should be as reliable as possible. But due to the systemic variation that exists in every group, there is always a certain amount of score variance in assessments that has nothing to do with the performance of the learners; rather, it's due to the design of the test.

If you're using standardized assessments to measure your UDL lesson, you'll need to attend to the test's reliability when you look at the results, especially if you're comparing the performance of one group with another. The good news is that reliability for informal classroom assessments is not as critical as it is for standardized assessments. Frankly, there's little

To err is human; to forgive divine.

—Attributed to Alexander Pope

Figure 4.3. Fire alarm.

opportunity or time in today's busy classrooms to give the same assessment multiple times to determine its reliability. What you can do to increase the reliability of your classroom assessments is to be as clear and consistent as possible. Give well-defined directions to all learners, check for understanding when you assign the assessment, and aim for consistency in how you evaluate the results. Moreover, be sure not to penalize learners with vague and imprecise testing techniques.

TYPES OF SCORES: ADVANTAGES AND DISADVANTAGES

Like Chandra, most educators want to use an assessment that yields scores that are quick and easy to tally and interpret. Some types of scores work well for measuring lesson goals, and some don't. Knowing more about the various kinds of scores will help you determine which assessment you want to use for your UDL lesson.

 **Take Note**

Many scoring techniques are based on the traditional statistical average used in standardized testing; however, the concept of learner variability indicates that there is no such thing as an average learner.

During lesson design, Rudner and Schafer (2002) recommend that edu-cators consider the advantages and disadvantages offered by the scoring tech-niques available. These techniques include

- Raw scores

- Percentage correct

- Proficiency scale

- Grade equivalent scores

- Percentile scores

- Standard scores

- Stanine scores

Raw Scores (Number of Correct Answers)

Raw scores are definitely easy to tally and accurately represent performance. You can also use them to illustrate progress over time. For example, administering an assess-ment before your UDL lesson gives you a baseline raw score that you can compare to a raw score achieved at the conclusion of the lesson. Generally, surveys and checklists itemize evaluation criteria, compute a raw score, and are an appropriate choice for UDL lessons. Raw scores for repeated measures—that is, assessments administered multiple times—are an excellent way to determine individual student progress.

What are the disadvantages? Raw scores are not appropriate for comparing per-formance student-to-student, because the difference between scores is meaningless without a frame of reference. If Barb correctly answered nine questions and Brad accurately answered five questions, you could deduce that Barb knew more answers than Brad; however, you can't assume that Barb is able to perform at a more complex level than Brad, because the difficulty of each question is not obvious in the total raw score. Brad could have answered the more difficult questions, and Barb could have missed them. If Brad takes the same test multiple times and gets a higher score each time, you can reasonably assume that his increased score means he's learned more.

Percentage Correct (Percentage of Correctly Answered Items out of the Total)

Percentages are easy to compute (especially if you use totals of 5, 10, or 20) and you can use them no matter how many items you have (e.g., 9 out of 10 = 90%; 3 out of 5 = 60%). Percentage correct (percentage) scores work well for measur-ing learning in a UDL lesson. In addition, you can assume that an individual student's increase in percentage scores from the first administration of a test to the second administration of the same test means the student's knowledge or skills have improved (e.g., pretest versus posttest scores).

What are the disadvantages? Similar to raw scores, percentages shouldn't be used to make student-to-student comparisons and various percentages don't reflect varying levels of difficulty. Even though Martin scored 80% accuracy on an assessment and Gracie scored 60% accuracy, it doesn't mean that Martin is performing at a higher grade level than Gracie is. Simply put, percentage correct scores only represent accuracy, not depth of understanding.

Proficiency Scale (Proficiency Rating)

A proficiency scale presents descriptions of knowledge or skills along a sequential continuum toward higher levels of performance. Proficiency scales are based on a standard, and each step in the proficiency scale represents a level of competency toward achieving the standard. As a result, educators often use proficiency scales to report individual as well as group progress. Many state accountability systems calculate proficiency ratings by mapping cutoff scores on standardized test scores against a descriptive proficiency scale. As an example, using 45 as the cutoff score for a standardized test, Richard, with a score of 40, did not meet proficiency; but Arlene, who scored 46, did. One type of proficiency scale that is particularly appropriate for measuring learning in a UDL lesson is a rubric. Rubrics contain descriptive performance criteria based on standards. To be accurate, the criteria must be clearly defined. More information on rubrics will come later in this chapter.

What are the disadvantages? One disadvantage of proficiency scales is they are only as accurate as the standards they are based on. And, it's important that proficiency scales closely align with the content you are teaching. Because teacher observation determines many proficiency ratings, consistency in teacher judgment is critical.

Grade Equivalent Scores (Grade Level)

Grade equivalent scores use a scale to estimate student performance. Sometimes educators report them as age equivalencies for younger learners. These scores are familiar and easily understood but frequently misinterpreted. Grade equivalent scores measure individual student achievement in relation to the achievement of large groups of students who take the same test. For example, Jake's score of 24 on the reading test is reported as equivalent to a fourth-grade level, because 24 was the average score of fourth-graders who took the test during its validation study.

What are the disadvantages? Because there is less sensitivity and limited accuracy for students who score at the high and low ends, it is inappropriate to use grade equivalent scores to determine individual student gains; and they are not useful for measuring learning in a UDL lesson or unit.

Percentile Scores, or Ranks (Percentage of Students in a Sample Whose Scores Are at or Lower than a Specific Score)

Percentile scores show rank in relation to national or local norms and are the most commonly reported results for standardized assessments. Although percentile scores are easy to explain, they are often used incorrectly and frequently misunderstood.

Figure 4.4. Test loophole cartoon. (From CALVIN AND HOBBES © 1995
Watterson. Reprinted with permission of UNIVERSAL UCLICK. All rights
reserved.)

What are the disadvantages? There is wide statistical variation within the
range of scores in each percentile rank, making it inappropriate to use percentile scores to determine individual gains, unless there are dramatic changes. For
example, Joe received an 85th-percentile rank on the local standardized test last
year, and this year he moved up to the 90th-percentile rank. He only correctly
answered two more questions this time, but it was enough to move his percentile
ranking up one level. On the other hand, Cathy answered five more questions
correctly this year than she did last time, but her percentile rank didn't increase
at all. It stayed at the 60th percentile. In order to move to the 65th-percentile
rank, she would have had to answer six questions correctly. Essentially, Cathy
missed the 65th percentile by one question. Percentile ranks are not effective for
measuring learning in a UDL lesson or unit and are most appropriate for looking
at the performance of large groups over a period of time.

Standard Scores (Scaled Scores)

Standard scores indicate how far the performance of individual learners
deviates from the mean or average score. Remember the myth of the average?

Other names for standard scores include *growth scale values* and *developmental standard scores*. Like stanine and grade-level scores, standard scores measure individual student achievement in relation to the performance of large groups of students who take the same test. Standard scores are distributed along equal-size intervals and can show individual growth over time. Assessors often use these to report the results of diagnostic assessments, such as psychoeducational evaluations. For instance, Collin's standard score of 112 on a recent standardized verbal comprehension test falls in the *average* range. His standard score for an assessment of perceptual reasoning is 126 and falls in the *high-average* range.

What are the disadvantages? Although standard scores can measure student improvement for diagnostic and accountability purposes, they are usually not specific enough to evaluate learning from daily UDL lessons.

Stanine Scores (Score Ranges)

Stanine scores report the results of standardized assessments and show performance in relation to the national or local average. *Stanine* is actually an abbreviation for *standard nine*. The ranges of scores are interpreted in this way: 1–3, *below average*; 4–6, *average*; 7–9, *above average*; with a score of 5 being *average* (the mean). Stanine scores measure individual student achievement in relation to achievement of large groups of students who take the same test. Jack's stanine score of 8 is considered *above average,* and Allison's score of 6 is considered *average.* Remember that a stanine score is a comparison with a statistical average, not an average of your classroom scores.

What are the disadvantages? Because they only give general information compared with a normed average, it is inappropriate to use stanine scores to determine individual gains, and they are not useful for measuring learning in a UDL lesson or unit.

The gist of it all is this: The best measures for UDL lesson planning are ones that look at individual growth over time, such as raw scores and percentage-correct scores from pre- and postassessments, and those that compare individual learner performance against clear expectations, such as rubrics or proficiency scales. Avoid using the others as measures for your UDL learning goals.

THE CHOICE: SUMMATIVE OR FORMATIVE?

There are two basic types of assessments to choose from as you develop your UDL lessons: summative and formative. Each has a different purpose and provides different information (see Figure 4.5). Let's explore how summative and formative assessments can meet your measurement needs.

Summative Assessment: Assessment *of* Learning

If the assessment occurs after the learning is complete and the results give a grade or provide a final measure of student results, it is summative (Rudner & Shafer, 2002). For the most part, educators administer and score summative assessments by using standardized procedures. Educators use summative

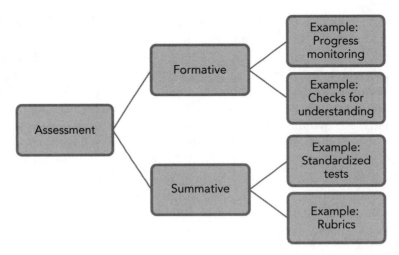

Figure 4.5. Types of assessments.

assessments to determine if learners have achieved a fixed set of standards in a specific area of study; therefore, they are assessments *of* learning. In addition, educators use them to evaluate the effectiveness of instruction. Rather than concentrating on the process of learning, summative assessments typically focus on products that teachers evaluate after completing instruction. However, teachers can administer summative assessments at intervals to establish snapshots of what learners know or are able to do at specific points in time. Examples of summative assessments include:

• End-of-chapter, -unit, or -term; end-of-year; interim; and benchmark tests

• Most standardized tests

• Online "games" with final scores (completed at the end of a lesson or unit)

• Final papers or essays measured by a proficiency scale

• Final projects measured by a rubric

What Is So Powerful About Rubrics?   Due to limited exposure, rubrics can be challenging for some educators. Let's examine what makes a rubric a powerful tool in more detail.

Originally developed to score performance tasks and products, such as essays, rubrics are scoring tools that educators have widely adopted for classroom assessment. A rubric describes what student work must consist of in order to get a certain score. It should be based on a standard and offer criteria or descriptions that are observable. Actually, performance standards are well tailored to representation in rubrics. Moreover, a rubric can divide the assignment into components aligned with standards and provide explanations of the components at increasing levels of mastery.

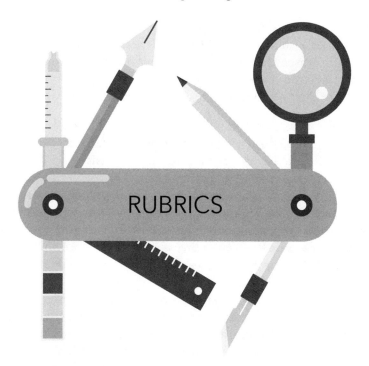

Figure 4.6. Power of a rubric.

All Educators Can Use Rubrics   Educators can use rubrics to assess an extensive range of student work (e.g., essays and other written work, individual and group projects, lab reports, presentations, exhibits, performances, physical tasks, portfolios of student work, artwork, internship experiences). They are therefore just as useful to college faculty as they are for preschool educators and just as meaningful to science teachers as they are to art and music teachers.

Eight Advantages of Using Rubrics   According to Suskie (2009), rubrics offer eight notable advantages. They

1. Allow teachers to evaluate complex tasks and strategic planning (executive function) skills

2. Clarify teacher expectations for students through detailed descriptions

3. Guide learners' goal-directed self-improvement

4. Inspire learners to perform at higher levels of mastery

5. Provide detailed feedback to learners

6. Allow teachers to score large or complex products faster

7. Allow teachers to assess student work with more accuracy and unbiased consistency

8. Reduce grading arguments between teachers and students or parents

Types of Rubrics   A rubric is typically depicted as a matrix that includes a set of criteria describing the expected quality characteristics of the product or process that you're assessing and projected performance levels matched to scores. There are two types of rubrics: holistic and analytic. Each type of rubric best addresses the evaluation and scoring needs for different types of learning goals.

Holistic Rubrics   A holistic rubric is just that: holistic in its approach. It includes an overall description of the entire product or performance rather than the components only. The performance criteria consist of a descriptive scale written in succinct statements, and evaluations of all performance criteria occur simultaneously. You would use a holistic rubric to score the overall quality, proficiency, or mastery of specific knowledge content and/or skills rather than evaluating each of the component parts separately. Holistic rubrics are also called *proficiency scales*. Because they center on overall performance, holistic rubrics are good scoring tools for summative assessments, such as a brief class report. Using holistic rubrics, educators can tolerate errors or weaknesses in some portion of the product or performance, provided the overall quality is high.

There are a couple of disadvantages to using holistic rubrics to consider. First, due to learner variability, assigning overall scores consistently can be difficult, because few learners meet a single description with accuracy. Also, they don't provide educators with detailed information about learners' strengths and needs. For an example of a holistic rubric, see Table 4.1.

Analytic Rubrics   Analytic rubrics allow educators to assess learners' work on a multidimensional level. Instead of scoring the product or performance as a whole, you analyze the separate parts of an assignment and score levels of performance for each component. Initially you will have several scores—one for each of the components—which you add together to derive the summed total score. As a result, you are able to give feedback to learners about their performance on each component and how they can improve. Analytic rubrics need to include criteria that objectively describe each component, such as *Essay contains no grammatical errors,* rather than subjective judgments, such as *Essay's grammatical construction is good* (Brookhart, 2013; Dougherty, 2012; Rudner & Schafer, 2002). You can use analytic rubrics for scoring both summative and formative assessments. For an example of an analytic rubric, see Table 4.2.

Formative Assessment: Assessment *for* Learning

Formative assessment is a process, not a particular test. Its purpose is to measure ongoing learning and help both teachers and learners make continuous improvements to student learning. The following six points summarize how formative assessment impacts achievement (Black & Wiliam, 1998; Marzano, 2010; Popham, 2008). It

1.   Provides feedback to both teachers and learners

2.   Is based on defined learning goals and criteria

Table 4.1. Rubric example A: Holistic rubric for class report

Score	Performance level description
5—distinguished	The learner clearly describes the topic and provides a strong rationale for its importance. The learner offers ample, specific information to support statements and conclusions. Preparation, organization, and enthusiasm for the topic are evident. Delivery is engaging. Grammatical use is consistently correct. Appropriate eye contact is used throughout the presentation. The learner uses visuals or graphics that add to the presentation. The learner clearly answers questions from the audience with specific, appropriate information.
4—proficient	The learner describes the topic and provides reasons for its importance. The learner offers an adequate amount of information to support statements and conclusions. Preparation, organization, and enthusiasm for the topic are evident. Delivery and grammatical use are generally correct. The learner uses relevant visuals and/or graphics. The learner clearly answers questions from the audience.
3—competent	The learner describes the topic and conclusions. Supporting information is present but not strong. Preparation and organization are evident. Delivery and grammatical use are generally correct. The learner uses associated visuals and/or graphics. The learner sufficiently answers questions from the audience.
2—beginner	The learner refers to the topic but fails to describe it well. The learner does not present conclusions clearly. Preparation and organization are lacking. Delivery and grammatical use are understandable but contain errors. The learner does not use relevant visuals or graphics. The learner gives only basic responses to questions from the audience.
1—novice	The learner's presentation does not include a description of the topic or its importance. Conclusions are unclear. Preparation and organization are not evident. Delivery is difficult to understand. The learner does not use visuals or graphics meaningfully or does not use them at all. Questions from the audience receive basic responses or no response.

3.   Actively involves learners

4.   Engages learners in self-monitoring

5.   Is grounded in the perspective that all learners can learn and improve

6.   Is focused on the *learning process*, emphasizing improvement of learning rather than grades.

Examples of formative assessments include:

- Progress-monitoring strategies

- Checks for understanding

- Frequent student surveys

- Periodic teacher observations

- Checklists and worksheets

- Pre-assessment of background knowledge

Table 4.2. Rubric example B: Analytic rubric for essays

Component/scores	4	3	2	1
Content	Answer is appropriate to the question. Content is factually correct.	Answer is appropriate to the question. Content may have one or two minor factual errors.	Content relates peripherally to the question and contains significant factual errors.	Content is unrelated to question.
Organization	Sense of order is clear. Essay begins with a thesis or topic sentence. Supporting points appear in a logical progression.	Essay may lack a thesis sentence, but student presents points in a logical progression.	Logic of argument is minimally perceivable. Student presents points in a seemingly random fashion, but all support the argument.	Lacks clear organizational plan. Reader is confused.
Development	Student develops each point with many specific details and answers question completely.	Some details and evidence support each point. All important points are included.	Details or evidence are sparse. Student answers question only partially.	There is no detail or explanation to support points. Development is repetitious, incoherent, or illogical.
Language use	Student uses technical or scientific terminology appropriately and correctly. There are no major grammatical or spelling errors.	Word choice is accurate. There are a few minor errors.	Ordinary word choice; avoids use of scientific terminology. There are serious errors (but they don't impair communication).	Student uses limited vocabulary. Errors impair communication.

 **Take Note**

Formative assessment is defined as "a process used by teachers and students during instruction that provides feedback to adjust ongoing teaching and learning to improve students' achievement of intended instructional outcomes" (Council of Chief State School Officers, 2008, p. 3).

Working Together: Formative Assessment and UDL Lesson Planning

The formative assessment process is integral to effective UDL lesson planning because it is a fluid, ongoing process that offers feedback to educators and learners prior to and during instruction. Educators who use formative assessments gather data, analyze it, and decide whether to change their instruction in response to their students' needs immediately—in the moment of instruction— or while planning a subsequent lesson. In addition, learners can use data from formative assessments to monitor and regulate their own learning. Using the information from formative assessments, students can evaluate how they are attempting to learn the content and then make appropriate changes. For example, after looking at her teacher's feedback in her Social Studies Learning Log, Kristin realized she was missing certain content. She decided to change how she was studying to concentrate less on facts and more on the rationales of key historical figures.

Let's examine two examples of formative assessment in more detail: progress monitoring and checks for understanding.

Progress Monitoring: Continuous, Data-Based Decision Making

You can implement progress monitoring with individual students or as a UDL lesson assessment for an entire class. Moss and Brookhart define progress monitoring as "an active and intentional learning process that partners the teacher and the students to continuously and systematically gather evidence of learning with the expressed goal of improving student achievement" (2009, p. 6). In other words, you should conduct continuous progress monitoring frequently (i.e., daily or at least weekly) to inform you about your learners' growth toward identified learning goals. With its roots in special education, the progress-monitoring process originally emerged in the 1980s and was linked with the response to intervention approach as a way to assess students' academic or behavioral performances, quantify students' rates of improvement or "responsiveness to instruction," and evaluate the effectiveness of instruction.

Special educators are quite familiar with the progress-monitoring process; but it is also valuable to other educators, because it delineates a method for gathering assessment measures (i.e., data) and a consistent format for using data to make educational decisions, such as adjusting your instruction. This data-based decision-making process includes these five steps:

1. Plan which measurement you need and how you will gather it.

2. Collect the data.

3. Analyze how this information illustrates learners' levels of performance.

4. Make decisions about how you will adjust your instruction based on these data.

5. Report the data and results of your decision making, if appropriate.

For example, Sharon uses progress monitoring to keep track of how well her first-grade students are able to complete reading-fluency probes. In another example, Marc, a school principal, measures changes in school behavior by charting discipline office reports. Both Sharon and Marc rely on their data to analyze growth and make decisions about student programs.

You may already be familiar with other terms that are related to progress monitoring: *curriculum-based assessment* (CBA) and *curriculum-based measurement* (CBM). Entire volumes address each of these measurement processes; and since it is not the intent of this book to go into depth about each of these, these short descriptions provide basic definitions: CBA uses direct observation of the learner's performance in the curriculum to determine academic progress; CBM is a formalized technique using probes or repeated measures to assess progress.

 **Learning Link**

To find resources on progress monitoring, take a look at the Center on Response to Intervention web site (http://www.rti4success.org/sites/default/files/whatthismeans.pdf) and Intervention Central (http://www.intervention-central.org/teaching-resources/downloads).

Checks for Understanding: Taking the Pulse of Instruction

You're ready to introduce new content or move to student application of content, but how will you know that your learners understand and are ready to move on? You can use checks for understanding or classroom assessment techniques (CATs). Checks for understanding and CATs are akin to quickly taking your pulse to check on your heart rate during a power walk. You can ensure that learners end up knowing what you want them to know at the end of your UDL lesson by routinely collecting information about what learners understand and are able to do—just like periodically checking your pulse helps you to end up at the desired end of your walk in a healthy state. Educators often use checks for understanding for formal and informal data collection, and the checks can be graded. CATs, however, are typically ungraded exercises to provide you with just-in-time feedback you can use to adjust your instruction or plan your next lesson. You can use CATs at any level and in any environment, and they have the additional advantage of increasing meaningful learner engagement in your lesson.

You are probably already using various checks for understanding and CATs now. In UDL lesson planning, they should be explicitly built into your lesson plan. While determining the assessment(s) for your lesson, scan the checks for understanding (see the CATs chart in Figure 4.7) and select those techniques that match your lesson and instructional style. Wise educators use them with such fluidity that they are unobtrusive and integral to instructional routines.

 **Reflection**

On a sticky note, write your thoughts about the purpose of informative assessment and offer one way you could embed formative assessments into your lessons. Share your thoughts with a colleague or peer. How similar or dissimilar are your ideas?

TRADITIONAL ASSESSMENTS WITH A UDL SPIN

Let's return to Chandra's use of quizzes as a tried-and-true assessment strategy. Sometimes educators such as Chandra get stuck using the same assessment format over and over because they are rushed in their lesson planning or don't feel comfortable employing different techniques that are not familiar. They develop UDL lessons but use traditional assessments to measure their students' learning. To truly make your lessons flexible and meaningful, your assessments need to reflect the UDL Guidelines too. At a minimum, your assessments should offer choices to your learners. If you're unsure of how to do this, consider first infusing UDL aspects into your traditional assessments for one lesson, one class, or one course. Eventually, adding a UDL spin to your traditional assessments will become automatic. Table 4.3 illustrates how to embed UDL features into traditional assessments.

ASSESSMENT ACCOMMODATIONS

Assessment accommodations are special adjustments that are allowed for a student with a disability because the disability interferes in the student's ability to show what he or she knows and can do. The accommodations permit a student with a disability to be able to participate equally in assessments. In other words, accommodations are not intended to provide an advantage but instead level the playing field so that the student with a disability is not at a disadvantage. Without accommodations, the assessment may not accurately measure what the student knows and is able to do. It's your responsibility to check the student's IEP or 504 Plan to find out what accommodations you are expected to provide. You should be sure to provide the accommodations during instruction as well as assessments so that the student is familiar with them in both situations.

Assessment accommodations change how the testing environment is structured (e.g., increased time and/or in a separate room to decrease distractions), how the assessment is presented (e.g., using headphones, in large print), and how the student responds (e.g., using an augmentative communication device, using a keyboard rather than a pen). Two final important points about accommodations are that they 1) should not alter what the assessment measures and 2) should not interfere with your ability to compare the assessment results of students with disabilities to other students' results.

Slates	Take 30 seconds
Pose a question to your learners and then ask them to write their answers on small dry-erase boards, chalkboards, index cards, or pieces of paper. You can quickly check understanding for your entire class.	Ask your learners, "What do I mean when I say, 'The Civil War was largely about states' rights'?" Have them take 30 seconds to write a one-sentence answer in their notebooks. Then they'll compare their responses with a partner's.
Thumbs-up/thumbs-down	**Fist to five**
Make a statement to the class or call on a learner for an answer to a specific question. Ask the class to indicate whether or not your statement or the student's response is correct by one of the following gestures: thumbs-up = yes, thumb flat = not sure, thumbs-down = no. You can quickly scan the room to determine whether the rest of the class knows the answer. This technique is not a reliable method but will give you an overview.	Suggest a statement to the learners. Then ask "Fist to five: How much do you agree?" At this point, students hold up five fingers if they strongly agree, no fingers if they strongly disagree, and any number of fingers in between to show variations of agreement or disagreement. Practice this technique with your learners to be sure they understand how to respond.
Signal cards	**Questions and probes**
After discussing or presenting new information, ask learners to hold up a note card to indicate their understanding. The note cards are different colors (e.g., green = Got it; red = Not yet) or have different symbols on them. You can also use them to gauge students' responses to true/false questions.	Educators frequently use thought-provoking questions to facilitate classroom conversations and enhance the content of their lessons. To ask questions that require more than recall, start your questions with "Why?" "How?" "In what way?" or "To what extent?"
Chain notes	**3–2–1**
Pass around an envelope with one question written on it. Each learner writes his or her response to the question on an index card and places it in the envelope and then passes it on to the next student.	Toward the end of class, ask learners to answer these exit questions: "What three things did you learn today?" "What two ideas are still unclear to you?" and "What one thing do you want to learn more about?"
Sign language	**Hold up two fingers**
Teach your learners a few words in sign language or fingerspelling. Ask the class as a whole to sign the first letter of the answer to a question or to sign the correct letter for a multiple-choice question (e.g., a, b, c, or d).	Have students hold up two fingers if they can tell you why a concept is like an analogous concept. For example: "Hold up two fingers if you can tell me why a name is like a rose."

Figure 4.7.   Checks for understanding and classroom assessment techniques.

(continued)

Paraphrasing	Say it in a sentence
Ask learners to compose a translation in their own words of a complex term or phrase from the content you have just presented.	Ask learners to summarize the content related to a critical topic into one succinct sentence. Scaffold their attempts with a guided format: "Who does what to whom, when, where, how, and why?" This works well as a small group or partner exercise.
Real-world application cards	**Create a question**
At the completion of a lesson about a key process, procedure, theory, or principle, learners suggest one real-world application on index cards. Collect the cards and analyze the answers. Share or use the student suggestions in a future lesson.	Toward the end of class or a unit of study, ask learners to develop one test question and model answer for a faux practice exam. Scaffold their responses by providing an example of typical course exam questions.
Appointment clock	**Think, pair, share (squared)**
Students find three people with whom to schedule appointments at the quarter, half hour, and 45-minute mark. At each point, students meet with their partners to share their thinking about specific questions.	A summarization strategy, students first ponder a question or problem; next they pair up and discuss their answers; finally they share with the rest of the class. In a different version, each pair meets with another pair to share their answers.

In contrast to accommodations, assessment modifications alter what the test is measuring and therefore change the expectations. For example, assessment modifications could call for reducing the number of items, presenting a reading passage using an audio-recorded version, or simplifying the text or content of a test. Specialized formats, such as braille, are commonly permitted assessment modifications (Thurlow, Elliott, & Ysseldyke, 2003). The results of a standardized assessment given with modifications cannot be compared to other students' results. Chapter 6 will cover more information about accommodations and modifications in reference to lesson materials and media.

SUMMARY

The third step in the UDL lesson planning process is matching your clearly defined learning goal with a flexible, meaningful assessment. Assessment is defined as the process of gathering and interpreting information or data about learner performance. To make sure that your UDL lesson matters, assessments should measure both learner products and the process of learning and should be ongoing and informative to both teachers and students. This chapter compared two types of assessments: summative (i.e., assessment *of* learning) and formative (i.e., assessment *for* learning). Educators can use either summative

Table 4.3. Traditional assessments with a UDL spin

Traditional assessment	UDL features	Scoring measure
Class reports—Educators use these as a stand-alone assessment or in combination with a written report. Learners present a report to the class to demonstrate their learning on a topic.	Provide multiple media options to add vital flexibility for those learners who fear talking in front of groups or have difficulty expressing themselves orally.	Proficiency rating scale Rubrics
Class notes—Notetaking is an important study skill, but it can also be a great assessment. For each class, assign one student to take notes for the rest of the class.	Encourage students to use a format of their choice (e.g., traditional outlining, slides, narrative, graphic organizer). Students share the notes with the rest of the class either through a class wiki or Google or Blackboard site or by making copies.	Rubrics
Admit/exit slips—Before, after, or at the beginning of the class, students reflect on their understanding of the previous class or prior night's homework. Ask questions such as "What's confusing you about _____?" or "What problems did you have with your assignment?"	Permit students to use multiple media to submit responses. Offer scaffolds, such as sentence prompts for those who may need examples.	Teacher analysis
Learning logs—Students record what they are learning, reflect on lessons, and receive feedback from teachers on any questions they may need clarified. Teachers read student logs and provide descriptive feedback.	Provide a model and use digital response modes to allow flexibility (e.g., a wiki).	Rubrics
Response logs—Students respond to lessons by asking questions, reflecting on lessons, collecting vocabulary, and composing thoughts about text.	Provide a model and use digital response modes to allow flexibility (e.g., web pages, digital formats).	Rubrics
Peer and self-assessment—Students share what they understand and what they still need to learn with each other.	Offer student choice for various groupings (e.g., pairs, small groups of three or four). Scaffold with checklist or graphic organizer.	Proficiency rating scale Rubrics
Quiz—Students respond to multiple-choice, true/false, or open-ended questions.	Present questions in various formats, including digital or auditory modes.	Raw scores Percentage of correct responses
Essay—Students respond to a prompt or compose a report on a topic.	Provide a model and allow a choice of multiple modes of expression (e.g., slides, video, audio support). Provide scaffolding through a graphic organizer for essay organization purposes.	Proficiency rating scale Rubrics

or formative assessments to evaluate learning in a UDL lesson plan, depending on what type of scoring measurement they are using. However, standardized assessments are generally not well suited to measuring learning in a UDL lesson. Certain scoring techniques (e.g., raw scores, percentages of correct responses, rubrics, proficiency scales, progress monitoring, checks for understanding) work well for UDL lesson planning because they provide meaningful information, are flexible, and can be used to assess individual student growth. If you have students with disabilities in your classroom, you should find out what assessment accommodations are listed in the students' IEP or 504 plans and be sure that students are familiar with those accommodations by providing them during instruction. Unlike Chandra, who tended to use an ill-considered assessment strategy, you can match your UDL lesson's assessment to your learning goal and make your lesson matter!

EXERCISE YOUR LEARNING: BUILD AN EFFECTIVE RUBRIC

To build an effective rubric, follow this four-step process:

1. Determine if you are looking for quality attributes (analytic) or overarching proficiency levels (holistic).

2. Define the evaluation criteria.

3. Break the assignment into three to eight meaningful, manageable parts.

4. Assign score points to descriptions.

Additional resources for building rubrics are available at:

- Rubistar: http://rubistar.4teachers.org/index.php

- The Eberly Center web site: http://www.cmu.edu/teaching/designteach/teach/rubrics.html

- Learning Outcome Assessment: http://www.calstate.edu/itl/resources/assessment/rubrics.shtml

CHECK-IN
10 Questions to Ask About Your Assessments

- How much flexibility is there in assessment item presentation?

- How accessible are the assessments?

- How relevant or meaningful are the assessments?

- How have you controlled for bias?

- How are learners able to monitor their progress?

- How will learners be able to correct errors?

- How are you offering choice or options?

- How are you offering incentives to enhance performance?

- How are you minimizing anxiety and distractions?

- How balanced are the assessment scaffolds?

UDL LESSON PLANNING IN ACTION

To observe UDL assessment in action, you may want to watch a brief video (approximately 3 minutes in length) that focuses on selecting accurate, appropriate, and meaningful assessments—the third step in the UDL lesson planning process. (See Video 4.1: Selecting Accurate, Appropriate, and Meaningful Assessment [go online to see the video].) You'll meet Chandra, a fourth-grade teacher who thoughtfully aligns her assessments with her learning goals. She knows that summative assessments are assessments of learning and that formative assessments are assessments for learning.

See how Chandra and other educators embed formative assessments into their lesson designs so that they can monitor students' progress periodically throughout each lesson. Look for examples of checks for understanding, such as exit tickets, Thumbs-up, Fist to five, and whiteboard responses.

REFLECTION QUESTIONS

1. To what extent do various types of assessments support expert learning?

2. In what ways can the results of summative and formative assessments measure student growth over time?

3. How do various assessments help you make decisions about adjustments you need to make in your instruction?

4. Which scoring techniques are most helpful in assessing UDL lessons? Why would you choose one over the other?

5. How can you use your assessments to tell the story of your students' growth? What data do you need to include? In what order?

6. In what ways could accessible, flexible assessments improve your students' self-reflection?

5

Choosing Wisely

Teaching Methods with a UDL Spin

This chapter highlights strategies for choosing instructional methods for your UDL lessons and discusses the importance of establishing routines within a UDL learning environment. Examples of how 10 educators infuse UDL features into their traditional instructional methods illustrate how educators can use the UDL Guidelines to design lessons to meet the needs of all learners.

For Roberta, choosing instructional methods for her lesson plans is a process of random selection. An English as a second language teacher, Roberta works with mixed groups of students, from fresh immigrants who know little English beyond "Hello" to U.S.-born English language learners who handle social communication well but need help with understanding complex academic language. It's hard to meet their various learning needs. For many years, she's either chosen a traditional board game or activity that students can do together or relied on suggestions from curriculum guides. Typically, after a brief joint activity, students consult the goals and assignments listed in their work folders and head off to different learning centers to complete worksheets or listen to audio examples. "My students have so many different needs and progress so slowly! I just don't know how to individualize and still plan for widely diverse groups. I feel like I'm playing lesson-plan roulette!" Roberta says to Karen, a fellow English as a second language teacher. She continues, "There has to be a better way to plan lessons that work for various students." In response, Karen suggests that learning more about UDL will help Roberta to thoughtfully choose methods for her lessons. "A way to choose wisely—that's what I need!" Roberta exclaims.

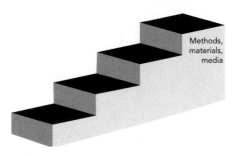

Methods, materials, media

Roberta has clearly defined goals for each of her learners, but she plans her instruction in a haphazard manner. She develops her lessons without a coherent decision-making framework for the methods she'll use to address her students' learning goals. As a result, she's missing the sense of connectedness she desires. The fourth step in the UDL lesson planning process is determining which methods, materials, and media will most effectively address your lesson goals while taking into consideration the variability of your learners. This chapter will focus on instructional methods. Chapter 6 will discuss materials and media.

The teaching methods that educators use can be as varied as the learning environments in which the educators teach and as different as the educators themselves. Every method can benefit from the UDL framework; though some more than others. The groundwork you've already done—developing flexible, clearly defined goals and informative, meaningful assessments—should logically lead you to certain instructional methods. This chapter will help you determine which ones will work best for each lesson by inspiring you to build on what you already do, offering you examples of what others have done and challenging you to consider new options. The first portion of this chapter discusses the importance of establishing classroom routines in a UDL learning environment. The second section briefly outlines 10 traditional instructional methods and shares how 10 educators applied UDL strategies to their instruction to attend to learner variability. Look for the language in italics to find connections between the UDL Guidelines and suggestions made throughout this chapter.

MAKING IT ROUTINE

Before discussing specific instructional methods, let's step back and explore an overarching strategy that fits into your lesson planning: routines. Effective instructional methods include routines that ease task completion and movement. For many reasons, they are a natural addition to any UDL learning environment. Essentially, routines are procedures, protocols, or rules for expected behavior. Some educators create routines unconsciously by establishing behavior rules or structures for handing in homework, seeking permission to leave the classroom, moving from task to task within the classroom, and asking for assistance. Roberta had established routines in her classroom. As a result, her students were able to anticipate that they would consult their work folders and then move to learning centers after they completed the joint activity.

If you want routines to work for you and your learners, you need to clarify a routine's purpose so that all of your learners understand it and to allow multiple opportunities for learners to practice or rehearse the routine when you introduce it. Remember that moving new concepts into long-term memory requires practice of that concept. Most important is to be consistent. Modeling the routine will be essential in the beginning, and occasionally tweaking it over time will keep it fresh. Adding a rhyme, song, or movement will make it fun and prompt your learners to quickly adopt it. Early childhood teachers often use songs or rhymes to teach routines to their young learners, such as "The Cleanup Song" or "Circle Time Rap." Many high school teachers, college faculty, and leaders of professional learning workshops use music or standard cues to alert their learners to the end of group discussions.

Consider which of the following typical routines you currently use: 1) roll call/attendance and lunch count, 2) alert or attention getters, 3) getting materials or supplies, 4) forming work groups, 5) lining up to exit, 6) changing classes, 7) responding to fire drills and safety alerts, and 8) dismissal. These routines primarily promote classroom efficiency and positive learner behaviors. Routines can also serve two other functions that relate to UDL design: 1) scaffolding learning *(heightening salience of goals; customizing display of information; supporting decoding; guiding information processing; highlighting patterns; building fluencies with graduated levels of support)* and 2) encouraging learner independence *(options for self-regulation; options for executive functions)*.

> If you're teaching today what you were teaching five years ago, either the field is dead or you are.
>
> —Noam Chomsky, Professor at MIT

INFUSING UDL INTO TRADITIONAL METHODS

Various instructional strategies serve different purposes. Traditional instructional methods tend to emphasize teacher-centered lectures and homogeneous learner grouping. Learners who struggle with lectures or who need more assistance bear the burden to adapt in order to achieve the lesson goal when traditional methods are used (Meyer et al., 2014). On the other hand, instruction that is infused with UDL strategies emphasizes interactivity, heterogeneous grouping, rich scaffolds and supports for understanding, and independent learning.

Although it's not practical to review every teaching strategy, let's look closely at how 10 different educators infuse UDL strategies into 10 commonly used instructional methods: 1) direct instruction, 2) question and answer (Q and A), 3) drill and practice, 4) discussion, 5) reciprocal teaching, 6) cooperative learning, 7) mental modeling and problem solving, 8) discovery learning, 9) inquiry-based or problem-based learning, and 10) case-based learning. The first five are teacher-focused methods, and the last five are student-directed methods. In this next section, I describe each method and then provide an example of how one educator infuses UDL strategies into that teaching method.

Direct Instruction and Lectures

Direct instruction is explicit or systematic teaching that primarily consists of lectures and teacher-led discussions (Metcalf, Evans, Flynn, & Williams, 2009). The lecture format is a long-standing method for traditional secondary and college instruction, particularly for large classes. It relies on the instructor to be the chief provider of content. Remember that Professor Brian O'Malley primarily used a lecture format with a follow-up discussion until he discovered UDL (see Chapter 3). One advantage of a lecture is that you can share a vast amount of information with a large group of people in a short amount of time. The disadvantage, though, is that, unless you are an extremely entertaining presenter, it can be unengaging for learners, because there is little opportunity for students to find personal relevance. Lectures are also less likely to lead to deep understanding, because learners usually don't act on the new content in a way that builds neural pathways for long-term memory shortage.

How Kelly Infuses UDL Strategies into Lectures

Dr. Kelly Wagner is a college professor who is familiar with UDL. She starts her lectures or teacher-led discussions with a provocative question, quote, or point of information to *recruit her learners' interest.* She often also begins with a KWL exercise (what do you *know, want to know, what did you learn?)* to *activate background knowledge.* She keeps her lectures to 15 to 20 minutes or less with opportunities for short peer-to-peer discussions or pause-and-reflect events every 5 to 10 minutes. (Remember the limits of working memory?) In her planning, she focuses on how she will *recruit interest, sustain attention, and optimize relevance.* By breaking her lectures into shorter time slots followed by a brief discussion, pause and reflect, or responsive exercise, she allows her learners a chance to act on the new information in some way, encouraging the movement of content from short-term memory to working memory and then to long-term memory. During momentary pauses, she asks learners to respond to questions by a show of hands, Fist to five, or one of the other classroom assessment techniques (see Chapter 4 for additional ideas).

Kelly always provides a lecture guide that organizes content into chunks for learners to *guide information processing* and includes a glossary to *clarify novel vocabulary,* an important strategy for the English language learners in her classes. Kelly likes to use slides or graphics to *display information in an alternative way.* She's careful to use bullets, graphics, and bold font on slides to *highlight critical features and big ideas.* None of her slides or graphics are cluttered or contain more than four to six lines of text. That way, she can make the text large enough to be visible from the back row (at least 24-point font). Kelly realizes that data displayed on slides is incomprehensible to most of her students. If she's discussing a table or sets of data, she also makes the table available in printed format so that students can see all of the information. Kelly makes her slides available before or during her lectures so that students can follow along and so that individuals with visual impairments can use a screen reader to translate the information.

Kelly's also careful not to use color (particularly red and orange) to convey information, because this makes the content less accessible to any learners who are color blind.

 **Learning Link**

To learn how to make your slides accessible, visit the National Center on Accessible Educational Materials web site at http://aem.cast.org/.

 **Take Note**

It's a good idea to plan your content for learners who are color blind, because many young learners don't know they are color blind and older students tend not to self-report.

Question and Answer

Educators have been using the Q and A format at least since the fifth century BC (Molenda, 2012). They often employ this method in tandem with lectures, as Q and A presumes that learners have enough content to participate knowledgeably. In addition to offering opportunities for recall and practice with subject matter, Q and A fulfills other purposes, including 1) assessing student comprehension, 2) *guiding information processing,* and 3) prompting *transfer and generalization* of content. Teachers use Q and A techniques in a variety of ways. For the most part, Q and A techniques can be categorized into three types: 1) teacher-to-student (the teacher asks questions), 2) student-to-teacher (students ask questions of the teacher), and 3) teacher-to-student-to-student (the teacher begins with a question, and then the responding student asks a question of a peer). In the case of the last two techniques, the teacher and students need to be sufficiently familiar with the content to be able to answer questions on the spur of the moment—a point to consider in terms of when this method may be most successful. Since Q and A requires learners to contemplate information in response to questions, it's most effective when used with students who are developmentally ready to offer reflective comments.

How Luis Infuses UDL Strategies into Q and A

Luis is a high school social studies teacher who often uses Q and A as his instructional method. He has established a number of routines that *reduce anxiety, minimize distractions,* and help learners to anticipate the sequence of the questions that might be asked. Applying UDL to his instruction, he uses *multiple ways to display models* of the types of questions that students can ask of him or each other, including the whiteboard, a wall chart, and placards at each group's table. His question models—based on Bloom's Taxonomy—are posted in the classroom via an easy-to-read wall chart (see Figure 5.1).

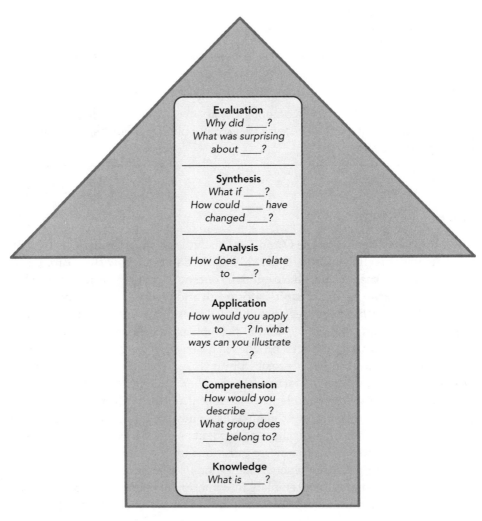

Figure 5.1. Model questions based on Bloom's Taxonomy.

Part of Luis's routine is a set of rules that limit the number of simple knowledge and recall questions that can be asked, focusing instead on analysis, synthesis, and evaluation questions. After he *provides students with content in a variety of ways* (e.g., text, readings, video, narrated slides, topical blogs), Luis holds an "interrogation" session, when students can ask him questions on the topic. *To foster collaboration and community,* groups of students develop the interrogation questions. *To optimize challenge,* Luis uses "call sticks"—which he refers to as the Question Lottery—to determine when each group will ask questions. The students enjoy the unpredictable aspect of the Question Lottery. Sometimes Luis *promotes high expectations to optimize motivation* by assigning a question type to a group; at other times he *optimizes choice and autonomy* by permitting students to choose their own question types. Learner groups are encouraged to *use multiple tools* to display their questions—prompt cards, slides, or online backchannels (e.g., https://padlet.com/). Finally, to *build comprehension* and *maximize transfer,* each student in Luis's class takes a turn at notetaking for the rest of the class. The notes are shared via a class wiki or through printed copies.

> A wise man can learn more from a foolish question than a fool can learn from a wise answer.
>
> –Bruce Lee

Drill and Practice

The format of drill and practice has its roots in behaviorist techniques, but educators have been using it in one way or another for centuries (Ebert et al., 2011). Underlying drill and practice is the assumption that learners have already been introduced to the content and need repetition to hone their ability to remember the information or enhance their facility with the new skill. Research indicates that learners tend to indefinitely retain knowledge or skills that they learned to a point of automaticity (Brophy, 2001). Consider how little effort it takes for you to recite the alphabet song, even though you learned it decades ago. The multiplication tables, state capitals, or periodic table of chemical elements are examples of content that teachers expected most of us to memorize through drill-and-practice exercises.

Drill and practice has a purpose: to move the novel content from working memory into long-term memory. To be an effective practice, the exercise must directly link to recent experience. You'll recall that Roberta used a form of drill and practice for her English as a second language sessions and wasn't satisfied with the results. Isolated fill-in-the-blank worksheets for content from a week ago or longer may be too distant from the brain's introduction to the information to successfully enhance knowledge retention. Therefore, educators should embed opportunities for practice within each lesson, and student attempts should receive timely, informative feedback.

Take Note

Practicing a new skill or applying novel information incorrectly can lead to student frustration. Also, the extra time it takes to reteach content can be frustrating to you.

How Kathleen Infuses UDL Strategies into Drill-and-Practice Sessions

Knowledgeable about UDL, Kathleen is a speech-language pathologist who relies on drill-and-practice methods to reinforce what the general education teachers have taught. Kathleen meets regularly with her students' general education teachers and maintains a running record of the topics they are teaching. She has copies of their curriculum guides and receives copies of their unit plans. She regularly coteaches or sees her students in small groups within the general education environment. In this way, she's able to ensure that her sessions are reinforcing recent instruction.

To *develop self-assessment and reflection,* each learner has a speech-language binder for his or her work products. In the front of the binder is a chart with each student's personal learning goals (written in student-friendly language). *To enhance their capacity to monitor their own progress,* learners routinely check their progress charts and report the goals or objectives they are working on as their session begins. To *minimize threats and distractions* during the session, Kathleen carefully sets up the learning environment so that students can feel successful. She offers *timely, meaningful, mastery-oriented feedback* to guide students in charting their own progress. Kathleen's primary focus is often *clarifying vocabulary, syntax, language structures, mathematical expressions, and other symbols related to recent general education classroom lessons.* She uses multiple materials to reinforce lesson content and *optimize relevance,* including authentic demonstrations, short videos, digital tools, and apps that are designed to reinforce new information. It's important to note that Kathleen proactively plans sessions that *gradually decrease the scaffolds and supports* necessary for learners to communicate effectively.

Discussion

Discussion is an age-old teaching method. By definition, a discussion is an exchange of information, opinions, and perspectives (Ebert et al., 2011). In the classroom, educators can hold discussions among large or small groups or structure them as peer-to-peer interactions, such as Think-pair-share, a commonly used discussion strategy between two peers. Discussions can be highly structured by pre-assigning questions or topics, or they can be more flexible and free flowing. They can be held person-to-person in real time or virtually via an online discussion forum or wiki. Properly supported, discussions serve to *foster collaboration and a sense of community* within the learning environment. Most state and national performance standards, including the CCSS, expect that learners will be able to engage in collaborative discussions and persuasive arguments in today's classrooms.

How James Infuses UDL Strategies into Discussions

A career-technology educator specializing in automobile technology, James finds that class discussions help to build comprehension of the technical manuals his learners must master. Many of his students learn well through discussions that synthesize information. He also realizes that improving his students' capacities to engage in productive, precise discussions can enhance their employability. As James infuses UDL into his lessons, he focuses on providing options that *promote high expectations and optimize choice, autonomy, relevance, value, and authenticity*. For example, after completing a chapter of their text, James presents a hypothetical problem that a client's vehicle could have and asks the students to discuss it. First, the students divide into pairs with one student (who plays the role of the technician) explaining the problem to the other (who plays the role of the uninformed client). Then learners share their experiences and observations with the entire class, *highlighting patterns, critical features, and big ideas* of their paired discussions. James draws this information out with discussion probes that he posts for all the students to view. As the students share with the class, James *provides an alternative for the auditory information, guides information processing, and promotes understanding across languages* by using a whiteboard to display specific points.

Reciprocal Teaching

Reciprocal teaching is a research-based, turn-taking dialogue between teachers and learners that is focused on developing reading comprehension. The four key strategies of reciprocal teaching are for students to 1) summarize the main content, 2) formulate questions about what they've read, 3) clarify ambiguities and misunderstandings, and 4) predict what may come next (Palincsar & Brown, 1984). In the beginning of the lesson, the teacher and students silently read the same text. Next, the teacher *highlights key strategies* and models them through a series of dialogues using think-alouds. For example, the teacher might read the title aloud and predict what the book or passage is about. Then, after each paragraph, the teacher might stop and provide a one-sentence summary of what that paragraph was about. After his or her turn, the teacher relinquishes the role of dialogue leader to one of the students and then serves as a coach to the dialogue leader, offering suggestions and *mastery-oriented, encouraging feedback.* As the role of dialogue leader passes to other students, the teacher gradually ceases giving comments to *promote the autonomy* of the student dialogue leaders, who replicate the strategies the teacher modeled.

How Margaret Infuses UDL into Reciprocal Teaching

A veteran reading specialist, Margaret relies on reciprocal teaching to build her students' reading comprehension skills, and she encourages all of the teachers in her school to use it with their reading groups. *To heighten its importance,* Margaret makes sure that each learner understands the purpose of improving reading comprehension using this strategy. *To optimize choice,* students preselect which paragraph or passage they will read. Margaret *supports decoding of the text* and *clarifies vocabulary, syntax, and language structure* through each of her think-alouds. The questions she formulates serve *to guide information processing and visualization* and *highlight patterns, critical features, big ideas, and relationships* discussed in the text. Margaret's also careful *to provide alternatives to her auditory directions* by providing learners with bookmarks that use pictures and graphics to illustrate the four key strategies she expects each student dialogue leader to use.

Cooperative Learning

Cooperative learning is a research-based instructional method commonly used across age levels and subject matter. Based on the belief that students learn best when working with others, it fosters a strong *sense of collaboration and community* within the learning environment. Experts in the field identify five key elements of cooperative learning: 1) positive interdependence, 2) face-to-face promotive (helpful) interaction, 3) individual and group accountability, 4) interpersonal and small-group skills, and 5) group processing (Johnson & Johnson, 2001). Teachers who employ cooperative learning promote the *development of self-regulation skills* by emphasizing that their learners need to take responsibility for their own learning during the group projects. To be effective, you need to take into consideration learner experiences and interests as well as learning goals when creating groups.

How Mary Jane Infuses UDL into Cooperative Learning

A significant portion of Mary Jane's job as an early childhood teacher is focused on helping her 4-year-olds learn how to work together in groups. She uses scores of routine group planning strategies, but one of her favorites is Numbered heads together. The children count from one to four, and then each group of four gathers together in a part of the room as a team. Mary Jane gives each team a set of objectives or pictures, and the teams have 5 minutes to "put their heads together" to answer various questions about the items. For example, one team's task could be to find all the pictures of animals that live on a farm and then organize them from the largest to the smallest. Mary Jane is careful to provide *various media* (e.g., photographs, real objects, manipulatives) to *clarify vocabulary*. She's invented a "Heads Together" rhyme to *guide information processing* for her oral directions. To *optimize choice* and *vary physical response*, she allows groups to choose their own workspace where they'll put their heads together. At the end of the group work session, each child evaluates the team's performance as well as his or her own performance by adding a colored plastic chip to the class teamwork jar if the team worked well together and adding a happy face sticker to his or her "I can" success chart. Mary Jane has found that this is a great way to encourage *collaboration* and *individual reflection*.

Mental Modeling and Problem Solving

Problem-solving methods, particularly those that involve mental modeling, focus on teaching learners how to visualize and solve puzzles the instructor poses. Whenever you ask learners to imagine or wonder how a situation might develop or what something might look like, you are using a form of mental modeling (Ebert et al., 2011; Johnson-Laird, 1998). In early grades, teachers often use self-talk, a form of mental modeling, as they demonstrate how they might think about or solve a problem before allowing the students to try. As the teacher explains the observations he or she makes and the steps taken to identify solutions, the learners are expected to visualize the teacher's actions and later replicate them in a similar situation.

During a lesson that includes problem solving or mental modeling, learners consider new information with regard to their personal background knowledge and experience, synthesize it, and then regulate their own learning by applying a problem-solving technique or model. By acting on new content in this way, they are able to more easily move information from working memory to long-term memory. Science instruction often includes the teacher modeling the steps of an experiment and then talking the learners through those same steps as they conduct the same experiment. Effective mathematics instruction also includes mental modeling during problem-solving exercises. Having your students verbalize their thinking as they engage in problem-solving assignments will *guide comprehension* and *support their planning and strategy development*. It also offers you an opportunity to assess their understanding.

How Nick Infuses UDL Strategies into Problem Solving

Nick finds visual simulations and mental modeling to be a critical element of his instruction as a middle school science teacher. In a recent lesson on kinetic and potential energy, Nick offered a variety of *media resources to illustrate* energy transformation and *build or activate background knowledge*. Students could *choose* to view a video about the transfer of energy, operate an interactive app demonstrating how energy is transformed during a roller coaster ride, or read a short article about the kinetic and potential energy of a golf ball. To *guide information processing*, Nick distributed a detailed guide and discussed the steps in developing a mental model *using multiple media*, including the whiteboard and passages from the science text. He then asked students to *construct and illustrate* their visualizations (i.e., mental models) of the energy transformation involved as various sized objects are dropped onto a chute. He encouraged students to *use multiple tools* to draw their mental models, such as a variety of web-based drawing tools. To *foster collaboration* and *optimize challenge*, students shared their ideas in small, diverse groups. The final steps in the lesson involved students observing a demonstration of various objects dropped onto a chute, comparing it to their mental models, and recording their observations in their journals. On their way out, the students completed exit tickets to *monitor their learning progress*.

Discovery Learning

Discovery learning is a teaching method that uses learners' experiences as the basis for new learning. Wiggins and McTighe (2005) refer to teachers focusing on "uncovering" rather than covering content. That is, learners uncover, or find, the information themselves as they engage in discovery learning. Typically, teachers provide the structure for the learning activity and then students document what they observe happening. Keep in mind that due to learner variability, each learner will experience the activity differently. Therefore, it's important to offer an organized structure for the assignment but not a rigid prescription that squelches curiosity and creativity. An advantage of discovery learning is that learners usually share a common experience, which helps to build *collaboration and community*.

How Colleen Infuses UDL Strategies into Discovery Learning

A librarian, Colleen intentionally embeds UDL into her discovery learning lessons. *To optimize individual choice* and *relevance,* she starts her lessons by asking students to brainstorm a list of two to three big ideas they want to learn more about. Then students compare their individual lists to a master list of topics that Colleen has created based on their curriculum and then align their big idea with one of the topics on the master list. In this way, Colleen helps her learners to authentically connect to key content while promoting *autonomy. To foster collaboration and community,* students can choose to form investigation teams with other students who are learning about the same or similar big ideas. Colleen's role is that of a discovery coach. She provides students with an "Investigation Guide" that *guides information processing, visualization, and manipulation* of the new information they will discover during their exploration. The guide offers a logical sequence for finding information on their big ideas, including library texts, sets of pictures and symbolic representations, available videos, and suggested web site lists that the students can explore to learn more about their big ideas. Available for reference are glossaries and dictionaries, including bilingual dictionaries, which *clarify vocabulary and symbols* and *promote understanding across languages.* At the end of class, learners present their learning *using multimedia* in a gallery walk.

> The art of teaching is the art of assisting discovery.
>
> —Mark Van Doren, American poet

Inquiry-Based or Problem-Based Learning

In contrast to teacher-directed learning, educators serve as facilitators in inquiry-based and problem-based learning, providing guidance and feedback as learners actively direct their own learning. It involves student investigation and hands-on materials. Educators provide learners with real-life problems that usually have a variety of possible answers (Cho & Brown, 2013; Larmer & Mergendoller, 2010).

Using a collaborative team approach, learners develop potential solutions to real-world problems using a defined problem-solving process wherein they 1) list what is known and unknown, 2) research the unknowns for clarification, 3) define a problem statement or driving question, 4) brainstorm ideas and model potential theories, and 5) present the best solution and their methods to a public audience. With this approach, each team member's participation is valuable, because each possesses different knowledge and a different background, skill set, and perspective. Moreover, each team member has a delineated role. For example, one team member is the facilitator or discussion leader, and another is the scribe.

Learning Link

To learn more about problem-based learning, check out a video from Edutopia (http://www.edutopia.org/project-based-learning-overview-video); the Bucks Institute for Education web site (http://bie.org/); or Education World's page on project-based learning (http://www.educationworld.com/a_tech/key-elements-project-based-learning.shtml#sthash.QkhRZxNj.dpuf).

**How Kevin Infuses UDL
Strategies into Problem-Based Learning**

Kevin's fourth-grade mathematics class engages in problem-based learning projects throughout the year. After Kevin presents a real-world problem and a rubric that describes the set of skills needed to solve the problem, the students *conduct a self-assessment* by reflecting on the rubric, evaluate their own knowledge and skills, and complete scavenger hunt templates that identify their strengths and interests. *To optimize autonomy* and *foster collaboration,* the class creates diverse teams by finding peers who match the skills and interests listed in scavenger hunt forms for each team. In the most recent problem-based learning project, students will investigate what it means to be fiscally responsible.

To build background knowledge, a local bank employee gives a short talk about the bank's saving program for children, *illustrating* the topic by *using multimedia* slides with graphics and a short video. Using actual coins and bills, she shows how the savings program calculates interest, which adds to their account balance. The teams first investigate how many students currently belong to the savings program by various means. For example, one team develops and distributes a schoolwide survey, collects the data, and compiles the information into a graph, while another team conducts spot interviews during recess and arrival time. Each team determines a driving question, brainstorms a list of ideas, *decides on a goal, develops a set of strategies and a plan, and monitors the team's progress.* All of the teams must identify reasons for saving and, using their mathematics graph, show how much money key items cost and how money grows in the accounts. The teams also *use multiple tools to construct* promotional posters and flyers to encourage schoolmates to join the saving program. Finally, *using multiple tools,* the teams share their project in a hallway gallery walk on parents' night. Throughout the project, Kevin *provides alternative and multiple options* for templates, tools, software, and other materials that *highlight critical features* and *guide information processing.* He is careful to build fluencies with the mathematics content and support students' communication skills by *offering graduated levels of support.*

Case-Based Learning

Similar to problem-based learning, educators who used case-based learning present learners with a problem to solve that's embedded in a story (the case). The educator suggests structures for how to analyze the problem and present solutions. To be effective, learners should have ample *choice* in how they decide to solve the problem. Case-based learning encourages learners to use their critical thinking skills (i.e., *executive functioning*) to formulate and test hypotheses, apply their knowledge to real situations, analyze actual problems, and develop strategies and solutions that can be evaluated for impact. Providing learners with a case featuring real problems to investigate is often very motivating. For most case-based scenarios, there is no single right answer (Herreid, 1998).

 **Learning Link**

These resources will help you learn more about case-based learning: UDL on Campus web site (http://udloncampus.cast.org/page/teach_case#.WTwGq-7pFwr0); and the National Center for Case Study Teaching in Science web site (http://sciencecases.lib.buffalo.edu/cs/).

 How Bill Infuses UDL Strategies into Case-Based Learning

Bill teaches at a popular community college. His courses are filled every semester with a mixture of students who want to become police officers, attorneys, crime scene investigators, forensic experts, criminal psychologists, and FBI agents. They come from all walks of life and bring with them a myriad of skills and experiences. For a long time, Bill has used case-based learning as a critical aspect of his course on criminal justice ethics. For example, as a final assignment, he *offers students a choice* of three scenarios to investigate. The scenarios are *available in multiple formats:* online, hard copy, and narrated descriptions. He assigns students to teams based on which scenarios they select. Each team is tasked with reading the scenario, defining the ethical issues evident in the case, determining a set of work strategies, and constructing a joint solution. Bill provides *templates for highlighting critical relationships* within the scenario, *a list of helpful resources,* and *essential questions to guide students' thinking (i.e., information processing).* He *promotes high expectations for all of the students.* He does not prescribe how the teams are to present their solutions to the case. Instead, he allows the teams to *construct their case solutions using multiple tools, media, and products,* including composing a joint paper, creating a slide or Prezi presentation, or producing a narrated video. He *offers mastery-oriented feedback* by evaluating the teams' work products against a well-constructed rubric.

EFFECTIVE UDL LESSONS

To address learner variability, effective lesson plans often contain combinations of the 10 teaching methods just illustrated. For example, a lesson plan might begin with a KWL exercise to activate background knowledge and recruit interest; then present content in a short lecture that offers multiple ways for learners to perceive and understand the new information; then move to a short Q and A to expand understanding and link new content with what learners already know; and, finally, end with a collaborative learning or inquiry-based learning assignment that allows learners to synthesize the information and apply it to investigate a set of questions or a presented problem. Table 5.1 illustrates a summary of traditional teaching methods with a UDL spin. Chapter 7 will illustrate ways that three educators combined various teaching methods infused with UDL strategies.

HOMEWORK AND PRACTICE WITH A UDL SPIN

According to experts, homework should vary by grade level and focus on work that learners can do independently (Dean, Hubble, Pitler, & Stone, 2012). In the traditional learning environment, the teacher uses class time to introduce and explore new content and skills and uses homework to practice or apply content and skills. For example, learners often start on a homework assignment in class and then complete it at home. Effective homework is not isolated practice. For example, assigning multiplication memorization exercises for homework when class work is focused on fractions is not fruitful. Since the purpose of homework is to help students reinforce movement of new learning to long-term memory and build automaticity, tasks should connect to recent instruction, resources should be available for students' review, and you should provide *graduated levels of scaffolds and supports.*

Homework aligned with UDL *optimizes choice* and *maximizes transfer and generalization.* Students should be encouraged to use homework pads or folders; and you should post homework assignments prominently on the classroom board. In addition, homework assignments should offer *mastery-oriented feedback* through immediate, descriptive feedback and should support learners in *developing self-assessment and reflection* skills.

A noteworthy exception to the traditional class–homework approach is flipped learning, a teaching method that has gained considerable attention recently (Bergmann & Sams, 2012). Flipped learning turns the traditional instructional paradigm around so that work at home focuses on direct instruction (e.g., students explore videos and readings) and classroom time focuses on interactive application.

 **Learning Link**

To learn more about flipped learning, see information on the Flipped Learning Network web site (http://fln.schoolwires.net/Page/1) and resources by flipped learning pioneers Jonathan Bergmann and Aaron Sams.

Table 5.1. Traditional instructional methods with a UDL spin (examples aligned with the UDL principles)

Lectures and direct instruction

Engagement	Representation	Action and Expression
Start lecture or teacher-led discussion with a provocative question, quote, or point of information.	Offer notetaking guides; suggest guiding questions.	Ask learners to record thoughts or questions in a backchannel or on index cards that can be passed to the teacher during a break.
Start with KWL (i.e., what do you *know*, *want* to know, what did you *learn*?) questions.	Offer glossary or dual-language dictionaries for novel vocabulary.	Insert opportunities during pause-and-reflect breaks for learners to use a physical response (e.g., show of hands or Fist to five).
Break lecture into shorter segments (5–10 minutes) followed by short peer-to-peer discussions or pause-and-reflect opportunities.	Provide short videos, slides, graphics, graphic organizers, manipulatives, realia (i.e., real items), or other alternative display options.	Use notetaking as a group assignment; allow learners to choose structure and media.
	Use lyrics, mnemonic strategies, and chunking.	

Question and answer

Engagement	Representation	Action and Expression
Permit students to choose which question type they will develop.	Use multiple ways to list the types of questions to ask.	As appropriate, assign question types to individuals or groups of students.
Share rubric expectations.	Provide a template for the sequence of potential questions, including routines, guides, prompts, whiteboard, a wall chart, placards at desks or tables, or graphics.	Provide multiple options for students to display their questions (e.g., prompt cards, slides, backchannel).
Arrange for students to develop questions in pairs or groups with a defined role for each student.		Offer process checklists and models of questions.
Use call sticks to determine when individuals or groups will ask questions.	Offer scaffolds for students who need them (e.g., selecting from an array of formed questions, sentence starters).	Make self-reflection templates available.
Vary locations and positions (e.g., four corners of room, teacher in the middle of a circle).		Allow wait time.

Drill and practice

Engagement	Representation	Action and Expression
Adjust levels of challenge as appropriate.	Connect content directly with recent instruction.	Establish personal learning goals for each session.
Allow students a choice of reinforcement.	Highlight critical features and relationships (e.g., similarities and differences).	Offer students a choice of media and tools.
Vary whether students work individually or in groups.	Present content utilizing multiple media and various formats, authentic examples, and models.	Provide students with opportunities to practice with scaffolds and supports.
Conference with students frequently.		Gradually decrease use of scaffolds and supports.
Provide timely, meaningful feedback.	Offer glossaries and dual-language dictionaries.	Pair content with music, dance, or art.
Provide progress charts or checklists for students to monitor their own learning.	Teach mnemonic strategies and use chunking.	Use checklists and progress templates.

(continued)

Table 5.1.   *(continued)*

Discussion

Engagement	Representation	Action and Expression
Connect discussions with relevant and authentic topics of interest to learners.	Use multimedia to summarize new content, draw conclusions, and identify similarities and differences.	To avoid unfocused or open-ended discussions, offer a problem for a focus or a topic to explore.
Offer students choice (e.g., which portion of the topic they will discuss or what role they want to play in the discussion).	Clarify abstract language (e.g., metaphors or analogies) with visual or authentic examples.	Provide discussion guides that facilitate learner planning and participation.
Provide a rubric with defined expectations.	Use role playing or simulations to build comprehension of others' perspectives.	Establish, model, and explicitly teach discourse rules (e.g., how to enter or end a discussion, control of volume and tone).
Vary grouping; use paired, small-group, and whole-class discussions with defined roles and responsibilities.	Use multiple displays for discussion starters and probes (e.g., whiteboard, blackboard, projected images).	Use procedural checklists.
Provide mastery-oriented feedback and checklists or other self-assessment tools for students to monitor their own learning.	Highlight common patterns, critical features, and big ideas that emerge through graphics (e.g., Venn diagrams).	Permit physical movement.
Use learner diaries or journals for students to track their learning.	Provide students with discussion guides that list key questions or topic headings to support information processing and promote understanding.	Offer alternatives for verbal and/or auditory information to allow all students to participate, including access to assistive technologies.
Monitor time with entertaining timers or prompts.		Use classroom assessment techniques (CATs) to monitor progress.
		Allow wait time.

Reciprocal teaching

Engagement	Representation	Action and Expression
Select reading materials that have personal relevance or value for learners.	Use word banks, glossaries, and dual-language dictionaries to build vocabulary skills.	Use planning and self-reflection checklists.
Allow students to select which paragraph or passage they will read.	Provide visual and graphic representations of key strategies.	Encourage students to use story webs and outlining and mapping tools.
Define group participation and roles clearly.	Model think-alouds that clarify vocabulary, decoding techniques, and strategies for comprehending sentence structure and abstract language.	Phase out support as students become more proficient dialogue leaders.
Offer students meaningful encouragement as they share comprehension strategies.	Highlight text patterns, critical features, big ideas, and relationships illustrated in the passage.	Offer, as appropriate, multiple tools for composition and writing.
Provide mastery-oriented feedback and self-assessment tools to guide self-regulation.		Provide alternatives for participation, including assistive technologies.

Collaborative learning

Engagement	Representation	Action and Expression
Share clear goals, group roles, and responsibilities; explicitly teach group collaboration strategies.	Use varied displays of content via media (e.g., pictures, photographs, diagrams, graphs, organizers, realia [i.e., real objects], manipulatives).	Provide guides and checklists to facilitate goal setting, planning, and participation.
Allow learners to select groups and workspace; use topics that have personal relevance or value for learners.	Provide word banks, glossaries, and dual-language dictionaries to build vocabulary skills.	Offer data collection and process templates and tools.
Provide timers and checklists for staying on task.	Offer multiple displays for group process rules and strategies (e.g., whiteboard, blackboard, projected images).	Use templates to guide self-reflection on work quality and completeness.
Offer models, prompts, and feedback for coping with frustrations, anxiety, and interpersonal tensions.		Provide multiple options for students to display their work products (e.g., slides, poster displays, video, story boards, comic strips, 3D models, text, presentations.)
Encourage learners to frequently evaluate individual and group collaboration.	Guide processing with rhymes, lyrics, mnemonic strategies, and chunking.	

Mental modeling and problem solving

Engagement	Representation	Action and Expression
Allow learners to select groups and workspace for designing and sharing.	Provide alternatives for visual simulations and illustrations by using multimedia (e.g., video, slides, interactive apps).	Allow learners to construct and illustrate mental models and visualizations by using a variety of media (e.g., text, video, drawing tools, mobile apps).
Provide topics that have personal relevance or value for learners.	Build background knowledge through real-world experiences and expert presentations.	Ask learners to record data and observations in journals.
Conference with learners to facilitate self-regulation.	Provide word banks, glossaries, and dual-language dictionaries to build vocabulary skills.	Provide calculation tools (e.g., calculators, geometric sketch pads).
Offer mastery-oriented feedback via verbal cues and prompts, stickers, and digital badges.	Offer process and procedural guides using multimedia (e.g., whiteboard, blackboard, projected text, organizers).	Encourage learners to use outlining and concept and process maps.
Use progress-monitoring tools (e.g., exit tickets, data, self-assessment checklists).		

Discovery learning

Engagement	Representation	Action and Expression
Allow students to select project topics and work teams.	Build background knowledge through real-world experiences and expert presentations.	Offer self-monitoring guides and templates for goal setting, planning, and data collection and analysis.
Provide rubrics and rules for discovery process and products.	Provide resources for investigation by using multimedia (e.g., text, video, graphic organizers, web sites).	Offer models for products.
Conference with learners to facilitate self-regulation.		Provide meaningful ways that learners can present or share their projects.
Provide mastery-oriented feedback and self-assessment tools.	Make glossaries and dual-language dictionaries available.	

(continued)

Table 5.1. (*continued*)

Inquiry-based or problem-based learning

Engagement	Representation	Action and Expression
Allow students to select project topics and work teams.	Build background knowledge through real-world experiences, field trips, expert presentations.	Permit physical movement.
Arrange for learners to interview real-world experts.	Use multimedia to summarize new content, draw conclusions, and identify similarities and differences.	Allow alternatives for information to allow all students to participate, including access to assistive technologies.
Provide rubrics for the team process and products.	Clarify abstract language (e.g., metaphors or analogies) with visual or authentic examples.	Offer self-monitoring guides and templates for goal setting, planning, and data collection and analysis.
Conference with teams and provide peer mentors to facilitate self-regulation.	Provide planning guides by using multimedia (e.g., text, video, graphic organizers).	Make models for products available.
Provide mastery-oriented feedback and self-assessment tools.	Provide word banks, glossaries, and dual-language dictionaries.	Provide meaningful ways that learners can present or share their projects.
Offer models, prompts, and feedback for coping with frustrations, anxiety, and interpersonal tensions.		

Case-based learning

Engagement	Representation	Action and Expression
Allow students to select project topics and to decide whether they will work individually or on a team.	Offer real-world case scenarios by using multimedia (e.g., text, video, graphic organizers).	Offer self-monitoring guides and templates for goal setting, planning, and data collection and analysis.
Provide rubrics for case-based products.	Consider using story webs or story boards to present case scenarios.	Provide models and examples for products.
Encourage learners to interview real-world examples.	Provide planning guides by using multimedia (e.g., text, video, graphic organizers).	Offer meaningful ways that learners can present or share their projects.
Conference with learners or teams to facilitate self-regulation.	Provide word banks, glossaries, and dual-language dictionaries to build vocabulary skills.	Offer alternatives that include access to assistive technologies.
Offer mastery-oriented feedback and self-assessment tools.		
Provide sufficient time.		
Vary types of cases.		

SUMMARY

This chapter included an overview of 10 commonly used teaching methods and examples of how 10 educators infused UDL into their teaching methods: 1) direct instruction, 2) Q and A, 3) drill and practice, 4) discussion, 5) reciprocal teaching, 6) cooperative learning, 7) mental modeling and problem solving, 8) discovery learning, 9) inquiry-based or problem-based learning, and 10) case-based learning. These examples illustrate that even though half of the teaching methods are typically teacher-directed learning and half are student-directed learning, you can use the UDL framework to address learner variability no matter which teaching method you use. You can facilitate your UDL lesson planning by establishing classroom routines that keep the UDL Guidelines in mind. In selecting teaching methods for their lessons, wise educators choose options that offer flexibility, relevance, and appropriately balance assistance with challenge.

CHECK-IN

Compare Teaching Methods and UDL Strategies

Fill in the Check-in in Figure 5.2 by indicating how familiar you are with each teaching method and UDL strategies you use or plan to use.

UDL LESSON PLANNING IN ACTION

To add to your understanding of Step 4 in the UDL lesson planning process, see Video 5.1: Traditional Teaching Methods with a UDL Spin (go online to see the video). This brief video (approximately 3 minutes in length) looks at traditional instructional methods with a UDL spin. You'll meet Roberta, an English as a second language teacher who infuses UDL into her lesson planning for her diverse group of English language learners. First, Roberta develops flexible, clearly defined learning goals and selects meaningful, formative assessments for her lessons. She's careful to choose teaching methods that allow multiple options and choice for her learners, allowing her to proactively avoid designing lessons that include learning barriers.

Look for examples of UDL strategies infused into traditional teaching methods, for instance, 1) activating background knowledge with a KWL exercise (What do you know, what do you want to know, and what did you learn?); 2) providing a lecture guide that organizes content into chunks; 3) using bullets, graphics, and bolding to highlight critical features and big ideas; 4) displaying models; 5) using call sticks to determine when each student or group will have a turn; 6) organizing a peer discussion with a Think-pair-share exercise; and 7) offering choice to students.

REFLECTION QUESTIONS

1. Do you feel it's easier to apply the UDL principles to teacher-directed or student-directed teaching methods? Why?

2. Do you feel some teaching methods benefit more from applying the UDL Guidelines? Which ones?

3. If you had to use only one teaching method infused with UDL strategies, which one would it be? How similar is it to the teaching methods you currently use?

4. Which routines do you feel are associated with different teaching methods? Which ones are necessary? Why?

5. What teaching methods besides the ones reviewed in this chapter do you use? In what ways could they benefit from the UDL principles?

Compare Teaching Methods and UDL Strategies

Teaching method	How familiar are you with this teaching method? 1 = novice; 3 = expert	List one UDL strategy you use or plan to use
Direct instruction—lecture		
Question and answer		
Drill and practice		
Discussion		
Reciprocal teaching		
Cooperative learning		
Mental modeling and problem solving		
Discovery learning		
Inquiry-based/Problem-based learning		
Case-based learning		

Figure 5.2. Compare Teaching Methods and UDL Strategies.

6

Adding Value

Materials and Media in a UDL Environment

Using the UDL principles as a guide, this chapter presents ideas for selecting materials and media for your UDL lessons that add value and discusses ways to organize your learning environment to facilitate UDL implementation. This chapter also clarifies key aspects of scaffolds and supports and the differences between instructional accommodations and modifications.

As a junior high special education teacher, Liz spends a lot of time adapting materials and creating accommodations for students in a variety of general education classrooms. She learned about UDL several years ago and is comfortable applying it to her own lesson planning. She'd like to help other teachers do it too, but she's not sure how. On the other hand, Annie, the technology specialist, moves in and out of classes all day, often with equipment and tools in hand. Teachers frequently stop by to consult with her, not just about technology but also about how to plan their lessons. Finally, Liz asks her one day, "How do you do it? What do you bring that I don't bring?"

Annie shares her secret: "Tools!" she says, smiling. Annie then explains that whenever she goes into general education classrooms or meets with teachers, she offers lists of resources, distributes lots of links and tools, and suggests ideas for materials and media that are easy to apply to lessons—especially UDL lessons. She provides every teacher with the UDL Guidelines graphic organizer and then follows up with lesson planning help and frequent check-ins. "I show teachers how to add value to their lessons with appropriate materials and media," Annie declares.

Liz perks up. "I'd like to help. Together, we could double the impact!"

When Liz is in general education classrooms, she's adapting materials and providing individual students with accommodations. This is important work, but she wants to meaningfully enrich the general education classroom lessons and learning environments with UDL too. Annie's figured out that she can use her knowledge of tools and resources to meaningfully help her colleagues with their UDL lesson planning. Teachers first come to her for tools and gradually start asking for help with lesson planning, even though she isn't an expert in their subject areas. She is a UDL expert and knows a lot about UDL tools. Liz will now join her in her effort.

Many technology specialists and special educators come to be viewed as their schools' UDL experts in the very same way: by first offering ways to adapt materials and tools to use in the classroom with students who have special needs, then creating resources to use in UDL lessons, and eventually presenting workshops on the UDL framework. Because many of the first conversations are about UDL tools, it's no wonder that a frequent misconception is that you need digital technology in order to implement UDL. Chapter 1 debunked this myth. It's true that technology can make instruction more accessible and engaging, but it's not necessary. Yet technology may be the first thing that intrigues educators about the UDL framework. It may be what first caught your interest.

 Reflection

What first intrigued you about UDL?

Choosing methods, materials, and media is the fourth step in the UDL lesson planning process. After you define your learning goal and assessment, you're ready to select your methods and materials. Since the last chapter focused on choosing methods, this chapter highlights ways to select the right materials and media for your UDL lessons, followed by a discussion of how to use the UDL principles to organize your learning environment. The final section includes information about how you offer assistance to students who need additional help through scaffolds, supports, accommodations, and modifications.

MATERIALS AND MEDIA THAT ADD VALUE

Both Liz and Annie offer important, appreciated assistance to others. Liz adapts materials and provides accommodations to individual students. In contrast, Annie provides teachers with tools and lists of potential media for their lessons. What she brings are resources that more students can use—maybe even the entire class. Together, Liz and Annie can offer teachers at their school a plethora of materials and media that will add value to classroom lessons and benefit all students.

Alone, we can do so little; together, we can do so much.

—Helen Keller

You should choose materials and media for your UDL lessons based on how well they help all learners achieve the learning goal. When you discover a new tool or app, it's tempting to try to push it into your next lesson. Occasionally that works. More often, materials or media thoughtlessly added to your lesson become distractions that cause your lesson to fall flat. For UDL lessons, choose materials and media that offer flexibility, relevance, and the appropriate level of assistance. In today's classrooms, digital technology can help overcome the limitations and barriers inherent in static, traditional, or text-based instructional resources (Meyer et al., 2014). For example, learners can independently use digital copies of handouts and text to increase font size, change the background color to improve visibility, highlight main points, use summarizing features, apply text-to-speech features, and use screen readers. In addition, free or low-cost digital technologies are increasingly available, making it impossible to offer a complete list here (see Table 6.1 for some examples). Remember that although *media* implies digital technology, low-tech options—such as drawing tools, sorting games, puzzles, display boards, charts, graphic organizers, concept and story maps, and manipulatives—can be just as successful.

 **Inspiration**

A mobile app developed by the Maryland Department of Education can help guide your selection of the right media. It is available for free download at https://www.appbrain.com/app/udlinks/com.hcpss.UDL.

At this point in your UDL lesson planning, you are probably looking for a tool or a couple of ideas of materials that will fit or enhance your lesson. You'll recall that Annie disseminated lists of resources and media tools to the teachers in her school that the teachers quickly scanned for ideas as they designed their lessons. What do you do if you don't have someone like Annie or Liz? Try turning the UDL Guidelines into questions. The questions will guide you in selecting materials and media that enrich your lessons. Table 6.1 contains some of the questions you might ask and a few suggestions. What other questions, examples, and resources would you include?

ACCESSIBLE EDUCATIONAL MATERIALS AND ASSISTIVE TECHNOLOGIES

All materials used in the learning environment should be designed or adaptable to be usable across the widest range of learner variability, which includes students with disabilities who may require specialized equipment and technologies and/or specialized formats (e.g., braille, large print, audio, digital text). If you are unfamiliar with assistive technologies and accessible educational materials,

Table 6.1. Materials and media examples (aligned with UDL)

Engagement questions	Examples	Web site resources
Are your materials authentic and relevant for learners? Can learners use your materials independently? Do your materials offer learner flexibility and choice? Do your materials minimize distractions? Do your materials foster collaborative work? Do your materials offer the right balance between challenge and frustration?	Clickers Polling and surveying tools Digital games Blogs Online journals and wikis Web-based discussion boards Backchannel apps Virtual video tours Web streaming	To make it personally relevant and engaging: BrainPOP: http://www.brainpop.com Infogram: https://infogr.am Voki: http://www.voki.com

Representation questions	Examples	Web site resources
Do your materials provide learners with multiple ways to access information (auditory, visual, tactile, and kinesthetic)? Do your materials include media that illustrate your content, vocabulary, and other symbols? Do your materials highlight big ideas, patterns, critical features, and relationships? Do your materials help learners to visualize or draw mental models?	Print-based materials balanced with other formats Visual or graphic representations Physical models or manipulatives Electronic archive of resource materials related to your content	To create or share stories: CAST Book Builder: http://bookbuilder.cast.org/ Storybird: http://storybird.com/about/ StorylineOnline: http://www.storylineonline.net/ To find content videos: History Channel Video/Audio: http://www.history.com/videos National Geographic: http://video.nationalgeographic.com

Action and expression questions	Examples	Web site resources
Have you considered the assistive technology needs of your learners? Are your materials physically available and easily accessed? Have you provided guidance on how to use the materials or media you've selected? Have you provided time for practice? Are your materials useful for analytical thinking, planning, and problem solving?	Digital voice software Visual, graphic, and video modeling Mind-mapping apps Goal-setting and planning tools	To share content and learning: Animoto: http://animoto.com Bubble.us: https://bubbl.us Capzles: http://www.capzles.com Make Beliefs Comix: http://www.makebeliefscomix.com Mindmeister: http://www.mindmeister.com ToonDoo: http://www.toondoo.com Voice Thread: http://voicethread.com Webspiration: http://www.mywebspiration.com/index.php Wordle: www.wordle.com XMind: http://www.xmind.net

work with the assistive technology experts, disability specialists, and special educators in your district, school, or institution. Dr. Joy Zabala developed a helpful student-centered structure for assistive technology decision making called the SETT Framework, which stands for student, environment, tasks, and tools (Zabala, 2005). (To download SETT resources, go to http://www.joyzabala.com/.)

 **Inspiration**

A helpful web site devoted to providing information about learning and attention issues, Understood (https://www.understood.org/en) describes assistive technology in parent-friendly language. You can also learn more about accessible educational materials from the National Center on Accessible Educational Materials web site (http://aem.cast.org/).

ORGANIZING A UDL LEARNING ENVIRONMENT

Both Liz and Annie keep their learning environments organized so that they can quickly access the materials and media they need. Some educators are naturally very efficient and neat; some are the educational equivalent of Charles Schultz's "Pig Pen" character. Take a moment to think about your learning environment or classroom. How organized is it? Does everything have a place? Can learners easily access the materials and media they need? Do you believe you use your instructional time wisely, or do you spend a lot of instructional time gathering materials and giving directions? Although organizing your learning environment may not rise to the top of your to-do list, it does impact the success of your UDL planning.

Two aspects you'll realize as you begin to apply UDL strategies to your lesson planning are that 1) initially, it may take more planning time, because teaching with UDL is different from traditional instructional practice; and 2) as your practice changes, you'll want to spend as much time as possible supporting learning instead of finding materials and redirecting students. Planning lessons for a learning environment that is organized with learner variability and the UDL framework in mind will ultimately save you planning and instructional time and facilitate your infusion of UDL into your practice.

Because the UDL framework is learner centered, effective UDL learning environments are too. Even if you teach in a lecture hall shared with others and you cannot redesign your physical space, there are a number of ways you can organize your learning environment to support infusion of UDL into your lesson plans. Not all of the UDL Guidelines apply, of course. Nonetheless, the following section describes ways to arrange a UDL-enabled learning environment using the language of the UDL Guidelines (in italics). Maybe you can envision additional ways?

Physical Layout

No matter what subject you teach or at what level you teach, your physical layout should be flexible, supportive, engaging, and organized in order to facilitate your UDL lessons. Student desks lined up in neat rows, one behind the other, and all facing the front of the room conjures up a lecturing teacher who paces the room—an image from yesteryear. Since you are reading this book about UDL lesson planning, it's probably safe to assume that you are not interested in a traditional, row-by-row physical layout. Instead, consider arranging seats in a circle or horseshoe shape so that every learner can see you and each other. A colorful, print-rich environment that echoes the cultural diversity of your learners will be an inviting, comfortable place to learn.

You can arrange your physical layout in alignment with the UDL Guidelines by following these suggestions:

Principle of Engagement

- *Minimize threats and distractions* by sitting in every seat to get an idea of each learner's view and then remove any visual or other barriers you discover.

- *Optimize choice and autonomy* by allowing students a choice in where they locate themselves and their belongings.

- *Foster collaboration and communication* by organizing the tables or clusters of desks to encourage discussions.

- *Facilitate coping skills* and *optimize development of self-reflection* by offering comfortable physical spaces that allow students to work quietly by themselves or in small groups. Add big floor pillows, beanbag chairs, or a small sofa and a carpet. Use a timer that all learners can see or hear. Keep learning goals, prompts, schedules, and checklists in consistent locations.

- *Promote expectations and beliefs that optimize motivation* by prominently displaying student work and highlighting their achievements.

Principle of Representation

- *Customize perception* by posting charts and posters so that all learners can view them. Make sure the font is large enough to be readable from any point in the room or allow learners to move closer if they can't see it.

- *Promote understanding across languages* by including bilingual or multilingual definitions for key information, such as schedules, calendars, announcements, and notices.

- *Guide information processing and supply background knowledge* by clearly labeling resource materials located on accessible shelves. Categorize and update them regularly. Provide access to digital and multimedia resources in organized areas.

Principle of Action and Expression

- *Optimize access* by establishing defined pathways that ease traffic flow in and out of the room and to and from major work areas.

- *Provide options for physical action, including various methods of navigation.* Learners should be able to move unimpeded throughout the room to locate materials by themselves.

Take Note

Consult with an occupational or physical therapist or a mobility specialist regarding your learning environment if any of your learners are blind, visually impaired, or have physical disabilities.

Learning Spaces

Attractive and organized student work areas or learning centers will increase the opportunity for learners to take responsibility for their own learning and for you to provide scaffolds for those who need them. For instance, in addition to an area for whole-class discussions, classrooms could include a quiet reading area; a quiet listening center with headsets where learners can play music, videos, or an audio narrated text; and a work table for hands-on projects. Flexibility and access are important.

Consider these recommendations, aligned with the UDL Guidelines, as you design your learning spaces:

Principle of Engagement

- *Optimize individual choice and autonomy* by providing bins, cubbies, or space for learners to keep their personal items and projects that are in process. Individual desks tend to get messy and are generally not good for storage of items that students need to hand in. As often as it's reasonable to do so, allow learners to choose where they want to work.

- *Encourage self-assessment and reflection and optimize motivation* by creating individual folders, plastic envelopes, or binders to collect homework and store work products. Include progress charts that learners can use to keep track of their goals and performances.

Principle of Representation

- *Offer alternatives for auditory information* by using bulletin boards and wall space to house routines, rules, and daily schedules. Prominently display your lesson goals.

- *Clarify vocabulary, symbols, syntax, and symbolic structures* by posting word walls, concept maps, charts, and graphics.

- *Support decoding of text, mathematical notations, and symbols* by providing easy access to books and media resources. In addition to alphabetical, you can organize them in a variety of ways, such as by topics, authors, or reading levels.

Principle of Action and Expression

- *Optimize access to tools and technology* by organizing laptops, tablets, iPads, accessories, and other media in accessible work areas.

- *Offer multiple tools for construction and composition* by creating work bins or baskets that contain paper and writing supplies (e.g., pencils, crayons, pens), tools for product assembly (e.g., scissors, rulers, glue, staplers), and other materials. Some teachers find it helpful to organize work bins that are designed for specific products.

Your Teaching Space

From a learner's perspective, wherever you teach from is your teaching space. Some teachers need a desk; some don't. Some teachers feel most comfortable locating their space in a traditional manner at the front of the room; others don't. Like Liz and Annie, some teachers travel from room to room or share space with others and have little control over their instructional environment. However, it is the rare educator who doesn't feel a need to have his or her own home base when teaching.

In a UDL-infused learning environment, you want your learners to be able to easily see or locate you. They should also have unimpeded access to any displays you are using, such as the whiteboard, blackboard, or projected slides. If there are physical, visual, or auditory distractions between your teaching space and your learners, it will interfere in their ability to *sustain effort and persist,* especially during times when you are presenting new information. You not only want a direct line of sight between you and your learners, but also you should be mindful about how well they can hear you. For example, you should face your students when talking. Avoid turning your head away from your students when you are talking, because the volume of your voice can decrease by almost half. The Maryland Department of Education created a UDL Simulator with Johns Hopkins University to illustrate a classroom environment aligned with UDL. Check it out at http://olms.cte.jhu.edu/olms2/simulator/web/simulations/69#!/scene/148.

 **Take Note**

Avoid talking and turning your back to your learners while writing on the board or reading a slide.

STRATEGIES THAT OFFER ASSISTANCE

No matter what methods, materials, or media you include in your UDL lesson plan, you should also consider offering various types of assistance to address learner variability. The most common strategies are scaffolds, supports, accommodations, and modifications. You may have heard definitions for these terms already; however, the definitions that you know may be slightly different from the ones that follow. Frankly, I use the following definitions because I feel they most clearly explain how and when to use each strategy. Let's unpack them.

Scaffolds

Scaffolds are instructional supports that are adaptive in nature. They help learners to achieve the learning goal(s) while gaining greater independence. Similar to construction scaffolding, they are temporary, assist when needed, and are gradually removed or faded out (Larkin, 2002; Lipscomb, Swanson, & West, 2004). Picture a young child learning to mount a balance beam. In the beginning, the instructor may hold on to the child's waist and physically lift her to the beam. As the student gains physical agility, the instructor may assist with a prompt or guiding hand but purposefully stand farther away, decreasing how much assistance she provides until the child is able to do it herself. The instructor is scaffolding the child's learning.

Why Use Scaffolds? Vygotsky (1978) suggests that educators consider the "zone of proximal development" (ZPD) in their instructional planning. The ZPD is the difference between what a learner can do by him or herself (i.e., actual developmental level) and what he or she can potentially do (i.e., potential developmental level) given assistance or guidance from the teacher. Scaffolds are a critical UDL teaching strategy that effective teachers use to bridge this ZPD gap.

In the language of the UDL Guidelines, scaffolds help you to create a learning environment that *minimizes threats and distractions* (Principle of Engagement), offers *customized displays for information,* provides *options for comprehension* (Principle of Representation), and enhances capacity for *monitoring progress* (Principle of Action and Expression). You can offer scaffolds to specific students or the entire class. Allowing learners to choose whether or not to use a scaffold encourages *self-regulation skills.*

 **Reflection**

In what ways do you currently use scaffolds in your instruction?

Types of Scaffolding Strategies The UDL Guidelines present a set of research-based scaffolding options to help you address learner variability (Meyer et al., 2014). Examples categorized by the UDL principles include:

- *Engagement*—offering task choices, adjusting levels of challenge, providing a selection of materials or resources, using process templates and checklists, allowing various groupings, and varying feedback and challenge

- *Representation*—highlighting big ideas or critical features; using concept or story maps, graphics, organizers, and diagrams; offering multiple examples, versions, think-alouds, and models; and illustrating with multimedia and tools (e.g., text-to-speech tools and audio narration).

- *Action and Expression*—offering templates for planning and creating products; providing prompts, hints, gestures, pointing, and cues for skill demonstration; using guiding questions for strategy development; allowing use of multimedia; and including word processors, mapping and organizational apps, and digital drawing tools.

Supports

The goal should always be to encourage learner independence; however, sometimes you cannot easily fade or only temporarily use assistance or adjustments. There are long-term supports that some students need to be successful. For instance, English language learners may need access to a bilingual dictionary or struggling readers may need a glossary, spell checker, or editing checklist to be able to participate in your lesson. The materials that Liz adapts, for example, are likely supports since they are needed by specific students over a long period of time. Of interest is that sometimes teachers discover that the same material or tool may be a support for one student and a scaffold for another. For instance, because of his learning disability, Cameron may always need to use a spell checker, but Crystal only needs it to verify new academic vocabulary when she's writing science lab reports. Learners are quick to drop assistance they don't need in a learning environment that is supportive and unthreatening, so there's no need to worry about your learners becoming dependent on assistance as a crutch. Wise educators balance the availability of scaffolds and supports with positive experiences, mastery-oriented feedback, and guidance toward independence.

Accommodations

Accommodations, another form of instructional assistance, have a different purpose from scaffolds. Educators provide these to students with disabilities and English language learners; and they are designed to level the playing field, because those specific learners cannot be successful without them. Not all students use accommodations—or at least they shouldn't.

The two main ways to discern the differences between scaffolds, supports, and accommodations are that scaffolds and supports are optional and can be provided to all students, whereas accommodations are required for specific students. If you wear eyeglasses, you know you can't see well without them, but with them you can see as well as someone who doesn't have a visual impairment. If you are nearsighted, you are required to wear them when you drive. They don't give you an edge over people who have normal eyesight; rather, they essentially equalize your ability to access visual information. This is the same rationale for deciding whether or not a certain learner should receive an accommodation. Since accommodations are identified in students' IEPs, 504 plans, or English language learner accommodation plans, you must provide them. When Liz is in a general education classroom, she can offer scaffolds and supports to any student who appears to need them. However, she *must* offer accommodations to the students who have IEPs or 504 plans. You must offer them too.

There are different types of accommodations. For instance, *instructional* accommodations include the use of graphic organizers, duplicated notes, chunking techniques, and extra wait time for processing. *Environmental* accommodations are changes or assistance within the physical environment (e.g., strategic seating), an alternative workspace or quiet setting, and proximity to the instructor. Examples of *assessment* accommodations include extended time limits; oral presentation of directions or test items; and use of a computer, word processor, or other device. To effectively employ assessment accommodations, use them during instruction as well as for classroom assessments so that learners will become familiar with them and be able to accurately demonstrate what they know and are able to do.

In some instances, the scaffolds you provide to all your learners in your UDL lessons will be identical or very close to the accommodations required by a student's IEP or accommodation plan. That's okay. When an English language learner or student with a disability can also use the scaffolds and supports that you offer to the entire class, you minimize the stigma associated with having so-called different learning needs. Think about how Jacque feels when his teacher describes the writing assignment for the rest of the class and then hands him the special graphic organizer designed just for him and tells him to use it. Contrast this with how he feels when his teacher announces that there is a graphic organizer that anyone can use and then nonchalantly hands it to him.

Modifications

Instructional modifications go beyond accommodations. They are alternatives or alterations in the curriculum content, type of instruction, or materials that are especially designated for students with disabilities. Modifications do not just level the playing field; they change it. They are student specific, and only those students who require them receive them. This is because modifications consist of adjustments that alter instruction or the learning environment to such an extent that the student's learning goals are different. For example, due to his significant cognitive disability, Miles is working on identifying numbers during his eighth-grade Algebra class rather than multiplying polynomials. Miles' curriculum content is modified, and many of the materials he uses are modifications.

 **Inspiration**

Do you want to learn how to create accessible materials in alternative or specialized formats? Visit this site maintained by the University at Edinburgh: http://www.ed.ac.uk/schools-departments/information-services/help-consultancy/accessibility/creating-materials.

SUMMARY

Choosing methods, materials, and media is the fourth step in the UDL lesson planning process. The previous chapter discussed various methods; this chapter presents ideas for selecting materials and media that add value to your UDL lessons. Planning UDL lessons may initially take more time, so maintaining a learning environment that you have organized with learner variability and the UDL framework in mind will ultimately save you planning and instructional time and facilitate the infusion of UDL into your practice. You can use the UDL Guidelines to help you arrange your classroom into a UDL learning environment. In addition, by turning the UDL Guidelines into questions, you can create a guide for selecting materials and media that are meaningful. Although *media* implies the use of digital technology, it's not a necessity to include web tools and digital resources in a lesson to make it a UDL lesson. (Of course, digital technology can make instruction more accessible and engaging.) As you design your UDL lesson, you will consider the types of assistance you need to include in order to address learner variability. The most common strategies are scaffolds, supports, accommodations, and modifications. A scaffold is temporary assistance that is gradually removed. Supports are offered for a longer period of time. Accommodations and modifications support students with disabilities or English language learners and are required by IEPs or accommodation plans. Accommodations level the playing field, whereas modifications alter the curriculum or environment to such an extent that expectations are different.

CHECK-IN

Scaffolds, Accommodations, and Modifications—Oh My!

Review Figure 6.1 and determine the level of adjustment that each of the following materials and media offer and whether you feel it is a scaffold, an accommodation, or a modification: Venn diagram, audiobook, large-print text, extra wait time, bilingual dictionary, and braille text.

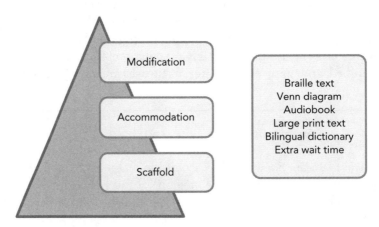

Figure 6.1.   Scaffolds, accommodations, and modifications.

UDL LESSON PLANNING IN ACTION

In addition to reading this chapter, you may want to view a video (approximately 3 minutes in length) that offers a brief window into choosing materials and media. See Video 6.1: Choosing Materials and Media (go online to see the video) to meet Daryl, a junior high school special education teacher who infuses UDL into his lesson planning. When he consults with other teachers about UDL, he suggests they turn the UDL guidelines into questions. He knows that all materials used in a UDL learning environment should be designed to be used by the widest range of learners, including students with disabilities and English language learners. Look for different examples of materials and tools used for engagement, representation, and action and expression, including digital technology.

REFLECTION QUESTIONS

1. What do you think happens when a teacher selects the materials and media first and then builds the rest of the lesson around them rather than starting with the learning goal?

2. How can a strategy such as chunking text content or using manipulatives be a scaffold, support, accommodation, and modification?

3. In what ways do digital media add value to lessons? How could they detract?

4. To what extent does a well-organized learning environment contribute to your UDL lesson planning?

7

Putting It Together

This chapter follows the lesson planning process of three educators who are applying UDL for the first time. Their lessons are examples of three different levels and subjects: Kindergarten reading readiness, middle school mathematics, and high school English. After examining the typical pitfalls of lesson planning and elements of a lesson, this chapter summarizes key points about UDL lesson planning using a road trip analogy and illustrates what UDL looks like when you're "putting it together."

It's a family matter. All veteran teachers, Laura, Pat, and Ray teach at different schools in the same district. Laura teaches Kindergarten, Pat teaches middle school mathematics, and Ray teaches ninth-grade English. Usually they don't share much about their teaching practice, even though they see each other every day. Laura and Ray are married. Pat is Ray's brother, and he's living with Laura and Ray temporarily while his house is being built. After attending the district's in-service workshop on UDL, the three teachers end up in a discussion over dinner. Laura admits that she's intrigued and would love to focus on applying UDL to her lesson planning; but she's so overwhelmed with the needs of her students that it seems like a lot to take on right now. Likewise, Ray says he's curious about whether or not UDL would increase student participation in his classes but simply doesn't know how to get started. Pat's interested too, but given that his curriculum and lesson planning format is set by the math department, he'd have to figure out how to infuse the UDL strategies into what he's already doing. "What if we help each other?" Laura suggests. "We all see the potential benefits; we have a basic understanding of the UDL framework; and each of us has a bank of lessons. We just need help putting it together!"

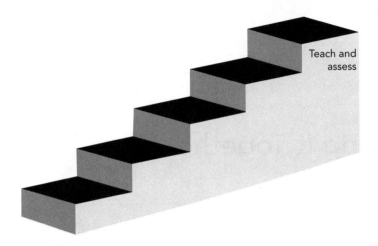

Feeling overwhelmed by the needs of her students, Laura's voiced a common concern. The last thing educators want to do is revise all their lessons using a new design. Ray's situation is a little different. He has concerns about learner engagement and wants to change his lessons but is hesitant about what to do first. And Pat is required to use a specific lesson plan structure that he can't change. What he needs is a way to embed UDL into his planning without altering his lesson format.

Maybe one or more of these scenarios is familiar to you. You may want to go all-in and change how you design your lessons from beginning to end, or you may want to go slowly, tweaking your lesson plans a little at a time. The good news is that either approach works! In this chapter, you'll find ideas to help you totally revise your lesson planning process as well as suggestions for how to fine-tune your existing lessons by infusing UDL elements. The goal of this chapter is to help you successfully put the suggestions from the previous chapters into action. As stated in Chapter 1, my hope is that as you apply the UDL framework to your lesson planning, you'll discover how UDL can become your instructional lens.

TYPICAL LESSON PITFALLS

First, let's expose an ugly truth: Poorly designed lessons cannot be saved by a smattering of UDL strategies here and there. Your lesson planning process is the fulcrum for effective instruction. Through their work with novice educators, Jones, Jones, and Vermette (2009) identified six common lesson planning mistakes:

1. Learning goals were unclear.

2. There was no assessment *of* learning during the lesson.

3. There was no assessment *for* learning (i.e., the teacher received no feedback of student understanding to guide instruction during the lesson).

4. The assessment didn't match the learning goal.

5. The teacher didn't know how to start the lesson in a way that engaged students.

6. Students were passive recipients of information.

Although previous chapters discussed all of these potential pitfalls, let's summarize this book's recommendations for addressing them:

- Define flexible, clear, SMART goals, drawing your purpose from appropriate standards.

- Plan for how students process information and learner variability using the UDL Guidelines.

- Provide your students with *experiences,* not passive teacher-talk, to build deep understanding.

- Use flexible, informative assessments that are matched to your learning goal.

- Balance assistance with challenge by choosing flexible methods, materials, and media.

The final chapter covers refining your learning and enhancing the learning of your students through self-reflection, an important aspect of putting it together as you create your UDL lesson plan and one that should permeate throughout all your lesson planning steps.

> Plans are nothing; planning is everything.
>
> —Dwight D. Eisenhower

A UDL LESSON ROAD MAP

As you start thinking about designing your UDL lesson plan, it might help to compare the process to the steps you take for planning your next road trip. The first step is deciding where you want to go. You'll consult a road map, making sure you have the precise address for your final destination. Any careful driver goes through a set of safety checks prior to a major road trip. For example, before you begin your road trip, you'll inspect the inflation of your tires, adjust your mirrors, and check your fuel and fluid levels. You'll also compare various routes for drive time and for potential problems you could encounter along the way. If you see that there is construction, barriers, or unrepaired highway along one route, you'll consider adjusting for the extra time or taking a different way. If you have a navigation system, you might input these considerations as you search for the right itinerary. En route, you'll periodically check guideposts and road signs to evaluate your progress and make sure you're headed in the right direction. Also, to ensure that all your passengers enjoy the trip and arrive safely at the final destination, you'll use a route that will offer services along the way for food, rest stops, and travel assistance. Once you arrive at your destination, you'll review the trip. Based on your experience, you'll make needed adjustments before you make the return trip or plan another one.

In many ways, lesson planning with UDL parallels this process.

Step 1: Define a Flexible, Clearly Defined Goal

As you begin to develop your lesson plan, your first step is to decide what you want your learners to learn about—your ultimate destination. As discussed in Chapter 2, you'll consult standards, a curriculum guide, or a syllabus to devise your lesson's flexible, SMART learning goal. In many cases, the CCSS or your state standards serve as the base for your UDL lesson's goal, and if you're teaching subjects beyond English language arts and mathematics, you'll look to the appropriate professional or performance standards for your purpose (e.g., American Library Association Standards for the 21st-Century Learner, National Arts Standards, National Association for Music Education Performance Standards, National Physical Education Standards, National Standards for Foreign Language Education, Next Generation Science Standards).

Step 2: Consider Learner Variability

Now that you know what your goal is, you'll assess the overall readiness levels, skills, and needs of your learners and the challenges of the learning environment. Do they have the background knowledge for this lesson? Do you have appropriate resources? How much time do you need? How much time do you have? Looking at your SMART learning goal, you'll anticipate learning gaps and barriers that may distract, frustrate, or confuse learners. You'll apply the UDL Guidelines to proactively plan for learner variability and determine what scaffolds are needed to engage learners and keep them on track.

Step 3: Select Meaningful, Informative Assessments

Your SMART learning goal will point you toward certain assessments you can utilize as your just-in-time guideposts. Assessments aligned with UDL will allow you to judge the pace and effectiveness of your instruction. Are you going too fast, too slow, or just right? Is the information clear or hazy? Do you need to stop and review certain content before moving ahead? Are they with you? Are they getting it?

Step 4: Choose Effective Teaching Methods, Materials, and Media

Your SMART learning goal will also help you determine which teaching methods, materials, and media will engage your learners and guide them to successfully achieve the desired outcome. Which UDL Guidelines will you address? Are you providing appropriate experiences to build deep understanding and make the learning memorable? Is there a balance between challenge and resources? Are your materials and media distracting or assisting your learners?

Step 5: Reflect, Adjust, and Enhance

After your lesson, you'll review the data you collected and think about your observations. What worked well? What will you do differently next time? Did your learners achieve the learning goal? What's next? Table 7.1 offers an analogy of road trip planning as an example as well as top questions to ask as you plan your lesson.

Table 7.1. Road trip–UDL lesson planning analogy

Road trip	UDL lesson planning	Questions to ask
Determine your final destination.	Develop your flexible, clearly defined, SMART learning goal.	Where will learners be by the end of the lesson? What's the clear purpose of this lesson? Is the goal SMART? Is the goal flexible or constricted? Is the goal meaningful and relevant? Does the goal allow for choice?
Before you begin, check the mirrors, tires, gasoline, and fluid levels.	Assess where your learners are at the beginning of the lesson by using a pre-assessment, a KWL-type exercise, data from a previous lesson, or your professional judgment to decide where to start.	What background knowledge and skills are necessary? What are learners able to do? Are learners working within their zones of proximal development? How does this lesson build on previous ones?
Anticipate diversions, detours, distractions, barriers, rough spots, and potential U-turns along the way.	Use the UDL Guidelines to plan for variability and potential learning barriers.	How will you present content so that it's accessible to all? Are alternative formats needed? Are they available? How will you clarify new vocabulary, language, and symbols? Are models and exemplars clear? How much scaffolding do students need? Can it be faded? What incentives will enhance performance? Do the tasks/materials/media cause anxiety or distractions? Is repetition needed? How will social dynamics affect engagement?
Look for guideposts and road signs to be sure you're headed in the right direction.	Use meaningful, informative assessments as your just-in-time guideposts.	What evidence will demonstrate that learners met the goal? Do learners have a choice in how they will show what they've learned? Do the resources appropriately balance the demands? How are learners able to monitor their own progress? Does the assessment cause or reduce anxiety? Is the assessment accessible? Flexible? Meaningful? Valid? Unbiased?

(continued)

Table 7.1.   *(continued)*

Road trip	UDL lesson planning	Questions to ask
Use the route that has the best places for sight-seeing and access to travel assistance so that all passengers enjoy the trip and arrive at the destination successfully.	Use teaching methods, materials, and media that engage your learners and that help them successfully achieve the goal.	How culturally and linguistically responsive are the goal, assessment, and materials? How personally meaningful and relevant are the lesson tasks? How accessible, authentic, appropriate, and safe are the materials and media? Will there be enough time to complete the lesson? Is there sufficient time for practice? Will collaboration enhance engagement and transfer? Do the methods, materials, and media allow for choice?
Review the route to decide what changes you need to make before you head out on your next trip.	Reflect on the data from your assessment(s) and observations.	Did your learners achieve the learning goal? What worked well? What could you have done differently? What needs reteaching? What should be the focus of your next lesson?

Key: SMART, Specific, measurable, attainable, results-oriented, and time-bound

 Reflection

What other planning scenarios similar to the Road Trip UDL Lesson Planning analogy come to mind?

LAURA'S LESSON: KINDERGARTEN READING READINESS

Varied Student Needs

To avoid feeling overwhelmed, Laura decides to focus on the UDL Principle of Representation for her next circle time lesson. Her class is very diverse. A couple of students are already reading at a first-grade level but need to improve their listening and social skills. Most of her students can recognize the alphabet and a few common words in the environment, like *stop* and *exit*. However, three students who are English language learners need support in understanding and using basic English vocabulary; two students with special needs have trouble listening for more than a few minutes without calling out in class; and several students are quite shy, rarely speaking during large-group time.

Infusing UDL into a Typical Lesson Structure

Laura typically develops her lessons using a five-stage structure: 1) anticipatory set, 2) instruction, 3) guided practice, 4) summary and assessment, and 5) independent practice. She adapts this structure to include a section highlighting UDL aspects. Here is an explanation of each element:

- *Anticipatory set*—In opening the lesson, the teacher creates an anticipatory set by focusing the learners on the goal, purpose, and relevance of the lesson by offering an interesting or engaging statement and by linking to a previous lesson.

- *Instruction*—The teacher clearly presents the new content, models a new process, offers alternative modes of interaction and communication (as appropriate), and uses checks for understanding throughout the session.

- *Guided practice*—As needed, the teacher provides scaffolds and guided practice, monitors and adjusts instruction, and checks again for understanding.

- *Summary and assessment*—At the end of the lesson, the teacher assesses student performance and achievement of the learning goal, summarizes the content by highlighting key points, and checks for understanding again.

- *Independent practice*—Students demonstrate their ability to apply new knowledge to a novel task.

Now let's look at Laura's process as she designs her lesson.

Learning Goal   Laura believes that the main focus of her Kindergarten curriculum should be on building language and social skills. After reviewing the CCSS, she selects a Kindergarten-level English Language Arts Literacy standard (i.e., CCSS.ELA-Literacy.RI.K.1). The goal she derives from the standard's purpose is to build reading comprehension skills by listening to a poem and answering questions about it. Laura's learning goal is flexible and SMART with embedded scaffolding (see below) that allows participation of all of her students. To address the learning goal, she designs a reading-readiness lesson focused on recalling information from a short poem and pictures in response to *who* and *what* questions and utilizes *I can* statements as a routine for sharing the goal with her students, and *We* _____ statements as a lesson summary. Here is her SMART learning goal: With prompting as needed, students will recall key details from a poem ("Rain, Rain, Go Away") and pictures to answer four out of five *who* and *what* questions.

Learner Variability   Laura decides to pair words with visuals to help her students make the decoding connection and build sight vocabulary for those students who are reading or starting to read. To scaffold vocabulary development for the English language learners, she includes gestures and facial expressions. She also pairs them with those students who are already reading and who can serve as models. For those shy students, she gives them multiple opportunities to respond during partner time and keeps a close eye on them. To maintain the attention of the students who have difficulty with listening in large groups, she locates them close to her and keeps her teacher-talk to a minimum.

Assessment   Laura decides to embed a simple check for understanding at the beginning of the lesson (e.g., Hold up two fingers). She uses a skill checklist to note how the students respond to the series of *who* and *what* questions during a Q and A and the group picture-card exercise.

Teaching Methods and Materials   Laura bases most of her instruction on stories and usually takes an eclectic approach in an effort to meet the varied needs of her Kindergarten students. The teaching methods she selects for this lesson are direct instruction, mental modeling, Q and A, discussion, and cooperative learning. As she reviews the UDL Guidelines for the Principle of Representation, Laura adds a representation option she's not used in the past: word cards paired with symbols (e.g., *Who, What, Listen, Answer*). To clarify vocabulary, sentence structure, and decoding of text, she chooses to use a choral call-and-response technique, physical response (clapping), and photos of students paired with their names. To promote important social skills and active engagement, she selects a student-to-student Q and A strategy.

Laura's Reflection

Planning and teaching this lesson led Laura to change her mind about using UDL as a lesson planning process. She realizes that she uses a lot of UDL strategies already, which makes embedding them purposefully rather than accidentally a reasonable shift in her thinking and that all of her students were fully engaged with no outbursts or behavior issues. "This is definitely worth doing!" she announces to Ray and Pat.

> Far and away the best prize that life has to offer is the chance to work hard at work worth doing.
>
> —Theodore Roosevelt

PAT'S LESSON: MIDDLE SCHOOL MATHEMATICS

UDL and Backward Design

The mathematics department in Pat's district requires all math teachers to use a lesson plan structure based on backward design (see Wiggins & McTighe, 2005). Pat could see definite parallels with UDL. But before he could change his lesson plan structure, Pat needed to discuss it with the chair of the mathematics department. As it turned out, his department chair had heard about UDL and was intrigued with Pat's idea. She agreed to permit Pat to redesign the current lesson plan if he would report on his efforts at a future department meeting.

Adapting an Existing Lesson Plan

The current mathematics lesson plan consists of these sections: 1) Desired Results (which includes standards), 2) Understandings (which includes essential

Laura's UDL Lesson Plan

Grade: Kindergarten

Lesson Goal: With prompting as needed, students will recall key details from a brief story/poem ("Rain, Rain, Go Away") and picture cards to answer four out of five *who* and *what* questions.

Standard: CCSS.ELA-LITERACY.RI.K.1

Estimated Time: 20 minutes

Teacher actions	Student actions	UDL strategies
Anticipatory set		**Engagement**
Sing: "Circle Time Song"	• Gather in a circle on the carpet (routine)	*Recruit attention:* "Circle Time Song"; Hold up two fingers
Ask: "Hold up two fingers if you have ever gone outside in the rain. What happened to you?"	• Sit and listen • Raise right hands (routine) • Respond to questions	**Representation** *Activate background knowledge:* Remind students of going out in rain and memories of a recent rainy day.
Display: rainy day symbol from the daily calendar		
Write: rain on chalkboard		*Support decoding of text/symbols:* Write and say "rain"; spell out R-A-I-N while writing.
Remind: learners of recent rainy day		
Instruction		**Engagement**
Tell: "Today we're going to hear a poem about a rainy day and listen for answers." Explain what a poem is.	• Repeat, "I can listen" • Repeat, "I can answer questions" • Sit and listen	*Guide appropriate goal setting:* State the goal and have students repeat.
Display: phrase cards *listen* and *answer questions* placed after *I can ____* sentence strip	• Close eyes and place a finger at their temples (routine)	**Representation** *Offer alternatives for auditory info:* Display *listen* word card, pages of book, picture cards, symbol cards for *who* and *what*; model gestures for *rain* and *away*.
Ask: "What's our 'I can' goal?"	• Listen to poem; look at book	
Describe: rain as drops of water that fall from clouds in the sky	• Brainstorm responses; respond to questions and listen as peers respond	*Clarify vocabulary:* Describe rain; show rainy day symbol.
Ask: "Think about what rain feels like for a moment."	• Clap at the end of each sentence	*Support decoding of text/symbols:* Display *listen* word card (word paired with picture of ear).
Read: "Rain, Rain, Go Away" by Caroline Jayne Church; display each page; use gestures for *rain* and *away*		

Figure 7.1. Laura's UDL lesson plan.

(continued)

Figure 7.1. *(continued)*

Ask five questions: "What's the title of this poem? Who is the poem about? What's Johnny doing? What does Johnny tell the rain? What could Johnny do if it wasn't raining?" Call on individual students and repeat responses.

Highlight big ideas: Display *who* and *what* words/symbols.

Highlight patterns: Clap at end of each sentence.

Guide information processing and visualization: Ask learners to visualize rain and what Johnny could do outside.

Guided practice

Tell: "Now it's your turn to read the poem. I'll say it; then you say it. Let's clap at the end of each sentence."

Second read: Read each sentence; stop; encourage learners to repeat each time and clap.

Repetition: "This time, let's see what the poem sounds like with your name in it." Explain that instead of saying, "Johnny," you'll pick a student's name (and picture) out of the "People We Know" bag and substitute that person's name.

Ask: After each repetition, ask, "Who wants to go out to play?" and "What do you want to do?"

Tell: "It's Partner Time. Let's make partners. Count off: one, two."

Ask: "Take turns telling your partner the 'Rain, Rain, Go Away' story. If you counted "one," you go first.

- Echo each phrase
- Clap at the end of each sentence
- Respond to *who* and *what* questions
- Count off in twos and turn toward partner (routine)
- Talk quietly in pairs, retelling story

Engagement

Optimize autonomy: Offer format for taking turns.

Foster collaboration: Have students do paired review of the story.

Representation

Offer alternatives for auditory info: Provide larger pictures if needed; display pictures on whiteboard or projector.

Offer photos of students on name cards.

Promote understanding across languages: Offer Spanish words for *who, what's happening,* and *rain.*

Action and Expression

Vary response: Model gestures for *rain* and *away;* allow pointing response if needed.

Build fluencies with graduated levels of support: Model book phrases; offer verbal prompts as needed.

Independent practice and assessment

Distribute: question bags that each contain 10 picture cards of students in the class to each partner pair

- Sit on carpet or go to tables with partner (routine)
- Talk quietly in pairs, focusing on pictures and answers to *who* and *what* questions, and bring completed materials to teacher at the end for review

Engagement

Optimize autonomy: Offer format for taking turns.

Foster collaboration: Have students do paired review of cards.

Tell: "Take turns with your partner to pull the pictures out of your bag. If it's your turn, pull out the picture and ask your partner, 'Who is this?' and 'What does ___ want to do?' Then it's your partner's turn to pull out a card and ask a *who* or *what* question."

Monitor: Move around the circle area/classroom to observe responses; note any difficulties answering questions on checklist.

Summarize: Collect the bags and lead the class in singing, "What did we do at circle time?" Point to *I can* statements (goals) and solicit answers: "We listened to a poem and we answered questions."

- Sing song (routine) and repeat *we* statements

Representation

Maximize generalization: Provide opportunities to apply vocabulary, to question, and to respond to a new task.

Action and Expression

Vary methods for response and navigation: Provide the option to move to another section of the room.

questions, skills, and knowledge), 3) Assessment Evidence, 4) Learning Plan, 5) Special Needs (which includes accommodations and modifications), and 6) Resources. Pat decides to combine the Special Needs section with a checklist for the UDL Guidelines and adds this new section alongside the Learning Plan section so that he can consider them all at the same time. Rather than adding these at the end of the lesson's plan, he believes his new thinking is more in line with the proactive planning associated with the UDL framework.

Opportunities for Action and Assessment

After selecting a seventh-grade lesson plan on proportional relationships, he decides to focus on incorporating the UDL Principle of Action and Expression and on building in multiple opportunities for assessment throughout the lesson. Even though his students are quite engaged during class, almost half the class failed his recent end-of-unit test. He believes one reason they did so poorly is because they need more practice at solving high-interest problems during class.

 **Inspiration**

If you're looking for a way to offer your learners additional practice in building logical reasoning skills, check out iSolveIt, a tablet-based set of puzzles designed using the UDL principles: http://isolveit.cast.org/home.

Let's take a look now at Pat's thinking methods for adapting his lesson plan structure.

Learning Goal   Pat selects a topic that is of interest to his seventh-graders: shopping. He incorporates relevant examples, flexibility, and peer-to-peer interaction to build deeper understanding. Here is his flexible, SMART learning goal: Given shopping examples, students will use proportional relationships to solve 10 multistep ratio/percent word problems with 90% accuracy.

Learner Variability   All of his students have had an experience shopping, but they have varied interests. Therefore, Pat creates four shopping wish lists that align with typical interests of this age group: technology, sports equipment, clothes, and music (CDs and musical instruments). Eight of his students are reading below grade level, with three of them at a second-grade level. To accommodate for the various reading levels, Pat incorporates multiple visual representations, pairing text and mathematical notation with pictures. He's confident that working in mixed-ability groups will provide good models for the students with weaker reading skills. He also decides to offer students multiple options for producing illustrations of their work in order to provide students with lower-level writing skills the scaffolding they need.

Assessment   Pat feels he needs to be more aware of what and how his students are learning so that he can adjust his pacing. He adds multiple opportunities throughout the lesson to assess what they know: Stand-up quick check, Fist to five, a team work-product illustration, and real-world application exit cards.

Teaching Methods and Materials   To build a deep understanding of mathematics, Pat often incorporates mental modeling and problem solving into his instruction. For this lesson, he adds a group cooperative learning project. As he selects materials and media, he concentrates on offering flexibility, choice, and multiple displays of the mathematical concept of proportional relationships. He adds a brief animated video on sales tax to enhance understanding and sustain student interest and offers multiple representations, including slides, a math vocabulary word wall, a Glogster poster, a spreadsheet of state sales taxes (displayed on a U.S. map using his whiteboard), a problem-solving checklist, and a group-product planning guide. He also provides a variety of options the students can use to create their final illustrations, such as an array of materials for creating posters as well as access to iPads loaded with apps for producing slides or short videos (i.e., Animoto, VoiceThread, PowToon).

Pat's Reflection

As he applies the UDL framework to his lesson plan (see Figure 7.2), Pat realizes that instead of limiting students to solving a few select word problems on worksheets, he can incorporate flexibility and choice into his lesson in a way that 1) offers meaningful opportunities to practice new content, 2) embeds needed

Pat's UDL Lesson Plan

Grade: 7—Mathematics

Desired results: Students will demonstrate understanding of proportional relationships and apply this understanding to a potential life situation.

Standard: CCSS.MATH. CONTENT.7.RP.A.3. Use proportional relationships to solve multistep ratio and percent problems (e.g., simple interest, tax, markups and markdowns, gratuities and commissions, fees, percent increase and decrease, percent error).

Enduring understandings (big ideas)	Essential questions
• A sales tax increases the cost of an item by the constant of proportionality. • A percent is another way to write a decimal or fraction that compares part to a whole, where the whole is 100.	• How are ratios related to proportions? • Why do some people pay more state taxes? • How can knowing about ratios save money?

Lesson goal: Given shopping examples, students will use proportional relationships to solve 10 multistep ratio/percent word problems with 90% accuracy.

Key knowledge—Students will know:	Key skills—Students will be able to:
• What the constant of proportionality is as it relates to sales tax • The relationship of percent to decimals	• Calculate the total cost of a purchase • Compose equations (e.g., cost = p (1.t) [p=price; t=tax]) • Solve multistep word problems by calculating percent

Assessment evidence	Accommodations and modifications
Stand-up quick check	__ Extended time
Fist to five	__ Oral directions
Accurate completion of tax rate team work product	__ Oral test items
Real-world application exit cards	__ Use of technology (AT) __ _____

Learning Plan

The teacher will. . .	Students will. . .	UDL strategies	Accommodations and modifications
Hook:		Provide options that	
• Begin lesson with dramatic statement "Who likes to shop?" followed by short discussion of what students bought	Raise hands	**Offer multiple means of Engagement** X Recruit interest/ optimize choice and autonomy	**Accommodations** __ Wait time X Organizer X Template

Figure 7.2. Pat's UDL lesson plan.

(continued)

Figure 7.2. *(continued)*

- Say, "Meet shopper Gavin. He has a problem and wants to move to another state"; display picture of Gavin and slide *What's Gavin's problem?*
- Explain that Gavin has shopping wish lists but thinks he's paying too much state sales tax

Quick pre-assessment:

- Display two proportional relationship equations (one for high and one for low sales tax)
- Have students do Stand up: "If you think equation A represents the sales tax in Gavin's state, stand up"; repeat for second example

Present content:

- Present brief video and explain proportional relationship sales tax
- Have students do Take 30 seconds: "Take 30 seconds to jot down your understanding of proportional relationships; turn to your right and share with your partner."

Assignment:

- Assign group task to determine which state is best for Gavin to purchase his wish list based on its sales tax. "Choose a state from the list and choose one of Gavin's wish lists. Work with your group to determine how much sales tax he will pay in five different states."

View picture and listen

Review equations and show their knowledge and judgment by standing

View video and listen to brief explanation
Note short definition and share with peers

Choose states and wish lists and work with small groups (three to four students); solve 10 proportional relationship word problems; use group planning guide as needed; add total costs of wish lists to class sales tax rate graph

---

X Enhance relevance, value, and authenticity

__ Minimize threats and distractions

__ Increase goal importance

X Vary demands and resources

X Foster collaboration and community

__ Increase mastery-oriented feedback

X Promote expectations and optimize motivation

__ Facilitate coping skills

__ Develop self-assessment and reflection

Offer multiple means of Representation

X Customize display

X Offer auditory/visual alternatives

X Clarify vocabulary and symbols

__ Clarify syntax and structure

X Decode text and math notation

__ Scaffold across languages

X Illustrate with multimedia

X Activate background knowledge

X Highlight patterns, critical features, big ideas, and relationships

---

__ Guided notes

__ Strategic seating

__ Alt. workspace

_____

_____

_____

Modifications

__ Adapted skill level

__ Adapted # of items

__ Adapted materials

__ Audio/video tool

__ Digital tool/AT

__ Personal assistance

IEP or 504 info:

_____

_____

_____

• Tell students they can choose how to display their work: line graph, Post-it graph, or pictograph	Work in groups to create illustrations of their work; use planning guide as needed	X Guide information processing and visualization
		X Maximize transfer
Summary and review:		**Offer multiple means of action and expression**
• Display graph of U.S. states by sales tax		X Offer varied response
• Have students do Fist to five: Select a few states with varied sales tax rates and ask students to judge how much Gavin/they would like to shop in each state	Respond with hand signal indicating their judgments (Fist to five)	X Provide access to tools
		X Offer multimedia for communication
• Have students use real-world cards: "Note one real-world example of how we use percent/proportional relationship on exit cards."	Indicate responses on exit cards as they leave and put cards in "real-world" basket	X Offer multiple composition and problem solving tools
		X Provide graduated scaffolds and practice
		___ Guide goal setting
		X Support planning and strategy development
		X Manage info and resources
		___ Monitor progress

Resources

Calculators, projector for presentation slides, word wall for vocabulary, poster made with Glogster, pictograph and video apps on class iPads, scaffolded group problem-solving checklist, group product planning guide, displayed spreadsheet of state sales taxes, Gavin's shopping wish lists (i.e., technology, sports equipment, clothes, CDs, and musical instruments), real-world exit cards

scaffolds almost invisibly, and 3) provides him with the daily data he needs to adjust his instruction. He tells Laura and Ray, "Using UDL lesson planning as a guide, I can add relevant practice and assessment. I can definitely do this!"

RAY'S LESSON: HIGH SCHOOL ENGLISH

Creating Engagement

Ray's colleauges and students know him as one of the best teachers in his school, yet he still struggles with a lack of participation of some learners. After the UDL workshop, he recognizes that he's actually bored with doing the same thing every year. His lesson plans provide plenty of content but not so much engagement. He decides to totally revamp how he plans his lessons, focusing on the UDL Principle of Engagement. To get some ideas about how

Table 7.2.   Find a lesson plan

Twenty-six lesson plan web sites

Annenberg Learner http://www.learner.org/resources/ lessonplanbrowse.html	A to Z Teacher Stuff http://lessons.atozteacherstuff.com/
CAST UDL Exchange http://udlexchange.cast.org/home	¡Colorín Colorado! (English language learner and bilingual) http://www.colorincolorado.org/ teaching-ells/common-core/common- core-videos-lesson-plans
CCSD Wiki-Teacher http://wiki-teacher.com/	Discovery Education http://school.discoveryeducation.com/ lessonplans/
Education World http://www.educationworld.com/a_lesson/	ESL Kid Stuff http://www.eslkidstuff.com/esl-kids- lesson-plans.html
Hot Chalk Education Network http://lessonplanspage.com/?s=%25	Jump Start (mathematics) http://www.jumpstart.com/teachers/ lesson-plans/math-lesson-plans
Kids.gov http://kids.usa.gov/teachers/lesson-plans/ index.shtml	Lesson Plan Central http://lessonplancentral.yolasite.com/
Lesson Plans.com http://www.lessonplans.com/	National Education Association http://www.nea.org/tools/LessonPlans.html
PBS Learning Media http://www.pbslearningmedia.org/	ReadWriteThink http://www.readwritethink.org/classroom- resources/lesson-plans/
Scholastic https://www.scholastic.com/teachers/ lessons-and-ideas/	Science Kids http://www.sciencekids.co.nz/ lessonplans.html
Share My Lesson http://www.sharemylesson.com/teaching- resources/	Teacher Created Resources http://www.teachercreated.com/lessons/
Teacher Vision https://www.teachervision.com/ lesson-planning/lesson	Teachers.net http://teachers.net/lessons/
Teachers Network http://www.teachersnetwork.org/	Teaching Community http://teaching.monster.com/training
Teachnology http://www.teach-nology.com/teachers/ lesson_plans/	The Teachers Corner http://lesson-plans.theteacherscorner.net/

to get started, Ray first investigates example lessons online. (See Table 7.2 for examples of online sites that offer lesson plans.) His investigation leads him to discover a plethora of ideas.

Here's Ray's process as he redesigns how he plans his lesson.

Learning Goal   Ray realizes that he lectures standing in front of the class too much. To increase student participation, he actually needs to give his learners the opportunity to engage. He reviews the CCSS and develops a goal focused on determining a theme or central idea in a text and using multiple media options to provide a summary of the text. This is Ray's flexible, SMART goal: Students will create a brief musical summary that demonstrates their analysis of connected details and at least two emerging themes in Kurt Vonnegut's *Slaughterhouse-Five* (measured by music product rubric).

Learner Variability   Even though he's teaching ninth-grade English, his students' reading levels span the spectrum, from one student with special needs whose labored reading is at a fourth-grade level to a number of highly gifted readers. To make sure they're familiar with the story, he assigns reading Vonnegut's *Slaughterhouse-Five* as homework. For those students who need an alternate version, he offers an audiobook and links to a video of Ethan Hawke reading the narrative. Throughout the lesson, Ray is careful to highlight big ideas from the text (e.g., by adding vocabulary to the word-wall poster of key words from the text). For those students who need vocabulary scaffolding, support for information processing, or help organizing their ideas, he provides copies of key text sections (chunked) that describe Billy Pilgrim's character, a vocabulary checklist, a product guide, and character and plot charts. Self-regulated learners and those with organizational needs alike can use the Music Product Rubric to guide their group work. To save time, Ray also provides a library of CDs and sample music organized by genre.

Assessment   Ray uses a quick thumbs-up/thumbs-down informal assessment at the beginning of the lesson and observes engagement as he moves around the room while the students work in groups. He has developed a Music Product Rubric to assess the final products.

Teaching Methods and Materials   To increase learner engagement, Ray decides to design a cooperative learning task that requires students to work together to create a joint product. Focusing on the UDL Principle of Engagement, he integrates the following strategies: First, he opens the lesson by highlighting topics that relate to learner interests and priorities. He then asks students to establish personal learning goals and clarifies from the beginning what will happen in the lesson. Ray builds and activates background information so that no one feels lost or left behind. He uses varied methods to support learner engagement and peer interaction throughout the lesson and offers choice to learners in how they will express their knowledge. Finally, Ray closes the lesson with a summary and discussion of what comes next.

Ray's Reflection

As Ray teaches his newly designed lesson on *Slaughterhouse-Five*, he becomes aware of how his role in the classroom has changed. He's no longer standing in the front as the "sage on the stage." Instead, he's a facilitator of learning, a guide moving from group to group, offering suggestions to individual students, and encouraging their investigations. Not only are all the students actively engaged in the lesson, but their learning is deeper and more relevant. Ray reports his conclusion to Laura and Pat: "UDL is the shot in the arm my teaching needed!"

> The secret to getting ahead is getting started.
>
> —Mark Twain

Figure 7.3 illustrates Ray's UDL lesson plan.

SUMMARY

As you apply UDL to your instruction and put it all together in your lesson plans, you may discover that UDL cannot save poorly designed lessons. To address the six common pitfalls in lesson planning (see Jones et al., 2009), consider these suggestions:

- Define flexible, clear, SMART goals drawing your purpose from appropriate standards.

- Plan for how students process information and for learner variability by using the UDL Guidelines.

- Provide your students with *experiences,* not passive teacher-talk, to build deep understanding.

- Use flexible, informative assessments that are matched to your learning goal.

- Balance assistance with challenge by choosing flexible methods, materials, and media.

This chapter describes how three educators applied UDL to their lesson planning, each focusing on a different UDL principle and taking a different route. Initially, they had misgivings and concerns; but once they tried it, they discovered that using UDL lesson planning enhanced their effectiveness and helped to resolve student engagement issues. To put it all together, follow these six steps of UDL lesson planning to design your lessons:

Step 1. Define a flexible, clearly defined goal.

Step 2. Consider learner variability.

Step 3. Select meaningful, informative assessments.

Step 4. Choose effective teaching methods and materials and media.

Step 5. Teach and assess student learning.

Step 6. Reflect, adjust, and enhance.

Ray's UDL Lesson Plan

Ninth-Grade English

Learning goal: Students will determine at least two emerging themes in Kurt Vonnegut's *Slaughterhouse-Five* and demonstrate their plot and theme analyses by creating a brief musical summary (measured by music product rubric).

Standard: RL.9-10.2.—Determine a theme or central idea of a text and analyze in detail its development over the course of the text, including how it emerges and is shaped and refined by specific details; provide an objective summary of the text.

Key objective(s):
- Identify and explain what is directly stated in the text and what is not.
- Connect the text to prior knowledge or personal experience that clarifies, extends, or challenges the ideas and/or information.
- Analyze events of the plot, main ideas, and universal themes.
- Use context to determine the meaning of words.

Opening

Recruit interest: Teacher asks students to visualize a time when they wanted to escape unseen to another time or place. Ask, "Why did you want to escape? Note on the sticky note how you felt (e.g., frightened, bored, anxious, overwhelmed, embarrassed) and place your sticky on the wall theme-chart."

Background knowledge preassessment: Tell students to think about the main character, Billy Pilgrim; ask if they think he's trying to escape. "Use thumbs-up if you think he's a time traveler, a dreamer, or a mad man." Note responses.

UDL Strategies
Engagement

- X Recruit interest/ optimize choice and autonomy
- X Enhance relevance, value, and authenticity
- X Minimize threats and distractions
- X Increase goal importance
- __ Vary demands and resources
- X Foster collaboration and community
- X Increase mastery-oriented feedback
- X Promote expecta-tions and optimize motivation
- __ Facilitate coping skills
- X Develop self-assessment and reflection

Representation

- X Customize display
- X Offer auditory/visual alternatives
- X Clarify vocab and symbols
- __ Clarify syntax and structure
- X Decode text and math notation

Methods

- __ Direct instruction
- __ Q and A
- __ Drill and practice
- __ Discussion
- __ Reciprocal teaching
- X Cooperative teaching
- __ Problem solving
- __ Discovery learning
- __ Problem-based learning
- __ Case-based learning

Structure

- __ Independent reading
- X Primary sources
- X Graphics
- __ Think-pair-share
- __ Fishbowl
- __ Jigsaw
- __ Pairs check/review
- X Small/large group
- __ Choral reading
- __ Simulation/role play
- Other _____

Assessment

- __ Collect and grade
- __ Check for completion
- __ In-class check
- X Rubric

Figure 7.3. Ray's UDL lesson plan.

(continued)

Figure 7.3. *(continued)*

Goal review: Review learning goal (displayed on board) and the purpose of the lesson and assignment: to identify plot and theme details from the text and work in groups to create a musical summary that represents the theme; ask each student to complete a personal goal sheet for this lesson.

During

Teacher guides students through the task process:

1. Based on their personal learning goals, students self-identify as either a friend of Billy (character expert), fellow traveler (plot expert), director (project manager), or music curator (product manager) and form teams, each team consisting of all four work roles.
2. Teams complete character analysis and plot charts, and decide the text's theme(s).
3. Teams determine what music would best represent the text theme(s) in the text and create a short (2-minute) musical representation.

Closing

1. As teams report out their themes, the teacher creates a cluster diagram and displays themes on whiteboard.
2. As students play their musical representations in a gallery walk around the room, the teacher grades the final products by using the musical product rubric.
3. Students review whether they achieved their personal learning goal and submit them on the way out of class.

___ Scaffold across languages

X Illustrate with multimedia

X Activate background knowledge

X Highlight patterns, critical features, big ideas, and relationships

X Guide information processing and visualization

X Maximize transfer

Action and Expression

X Offer varied responses

X Provide access to tools

X Offer multimedia for communication

X Offer multiple composition and problem-solving tools

X Provide graduated scaffolds and practice

___ Guide goal setting

X Support planning and strategy development

X Manage info and resources

X Monitor progress

X Checklist

___ Peer/self-assessment

___ Journal/learning log

___ Portfolio

___ Constructed response

___ Quiz

___ Test

X Presentation

___ Performance assessment

X Informal assessment

X Exit slip

___ Other

Accommodations

(Based on IEP/504)
___ Text audio recording
_____
_____
_____
_____

Materials:

• Copies of the text, chunked text, audiobooks, and links to video (as needed)
• Sticky notes for each student
• Product Guide, posted on board
• Vocabulary checklist; word wall poster
• Character and plot charts
• CDs; sample music; access to music excerpts
• Music product rubric

CHECK-IN

Lesson Analysis

Select one of your lessons or a lesson that you find online. (See Table 7.2 for sample lesson plan sites.) Use the chart in Figure 7.4 to evaluate how the lesson aligns with the UDL lesson planning process.

Check-In: Lesson Analysis

LESSON TITLE:
WEB LOCATION (if applicable):

Lesson analysis criteria	Yes	No	How would you enhance this lesson?
1. The lesson goal is flexible, clearly defined, and SMART.			
2. The lesson plan considers learner variability, including learning gaps and barriers.			
3. The lesson includes meaningful, informative assessments of learning that is aligned to the lesson goal.			
4. The lesson addresses UDL Guidelines by using appropriate, engaging, meaningful, and goal-oriented teaching methods, materials, and media. a. The lesson engages learners. b. The learners are able to access and understand content. c. The lesson provides opportunities for learners to apply content and show what they know and are able to do.			
5. The lesson plan includes assessment for learning, offering an opportunity to collect relevant data about learner progress for teacher and student reflection.			

Figure 7.4.   Check-In: Lesson Analysis.

REFLECTION QUESTIONS

1. To what extent do you agree with this statement: Teachers need to retreat from breadth of coverage in order to allow time to build a deeper understanding of content. What role does effective UDL lesson planning play in your response?

2. Would you describe UDL lesson planning as more than just good teaching? Why or why not?

3. Homework is generally considered to be independent practice that occurs outside of class time. How challenging would it be to align homework assignments with the UDL Guidelines?

4. How are checking for understanding and guided practice different? In what ways can UDL lesson planning enhance your use of either or both of these instructional elements?

8

Reflecting on Expertise

Reflecting on your UDL lesson is the final step in the UDL lesson planning process. This chapter defines expert learning, offers self-reflection strategies for both educators and their students, discusses how professional learning communities can enhance your practice, and suggests using a novice-to-expert scale to monitor progress.

Daryl is the ultimate UDL cheerleader. As he talks with his colleagues about his lessons, his enthusiasm is infectious. One day, Molly and Brenda ask Daryl to show them how he plans his UDL lessons. When they meet, Daryl is surprised by how differently they respond. A new teacher, Molly asks lots of questions about each of the steps in Daryl's UDL lesson planning process and takes detailed notes. In contrast, Brenda doesn't ask any questions. She listens intently, almost critically, restating a few things that Daryl says in her own words. After their session, Daryl thinks, Molly's so excited about UDL. She's going to start right away to change her lesson planning. But I don't think Brenda's convinced that UDL will make a difference in her practice. She's been teaching a long time and probably doesn't feel a need to make any changes. Weeks later, Molly admits that she tried Daryl's method but got confused and gave up. On the other hand, Brenda stuns Daryl when she announces that using a UDL lens is a great addition to her lesson planning process. "It's a fabulous way to take my teaching to the next level!" Brenda exclaims. Daryl walks away, wondering how he misread their reactions.

Daryl is surprised by how differently Molly and Brenda respond to his ideas. He could take a variability perspective and chalk up the discrepancy to learner variability—which would be accurate. Just like their students, educators are learners too, and they vary in their knowledge, skills, interests, and perspectives. Then again, there is another rationale. Molly and Brenda are at different points in their careers. Molly is a novice who sees her practice as a series of procedures. She's concurrently learning about many aspects of her practice, and it's easy for her to get lost in the weeds. In contrast, Brenda is an expert who views her instruction holistically. She's able to discern what's salient and what isn't and quickly zeros in on what fits with her practice. In other words, she cuts through the weeds to find the kernels that will make a difference.

Effective teachers are constantly learning. In fact, they typically are expert learners who continually enhance their expertise through self-reflection. Interestingly, Daryl, Molly, and Brenda can all be expert learners yet not necessarily expert teachers. Note that these two constructs are not equivalent. This chapter discusses the final, vital step in the UDL planning process: lesson reflection. It also explores the development of expertise and critical characteristics of expert learning and self-reflection as they apply to UDL lesson planning. As you move ahead, it's important to keep in mind that these concepts apply to both educators and their learners.

EXPERT LEARNING

Let's start by clarifying the characteristics of expert learning. In many ways, applying the UDL framework successfully to their practice requires educators to be expert learners (i.e., knowledgeable, goal directed, and motivated to change their instruction). In addition, one of the primary goals of applying UDL to your

PURPOSEFUL & MOTIVATED LEARNERS	RESOURCEFUL & KNOWLEDGEABLE LEARNERS	STRATEGIC & GOAL-DIRECTED LEARNERS
+ Are eager for new learning and are motivated by the mastery of learning itself	+ Bring considerable prior knowledge to new learning	+ Formulate plans for learning
+ Are goal-directed in their learning	+ Activate that prior knowledge to identify, organize, prioritize, and assimilate new information	+ Devise effective strategies and tactics to optimize learning
+ Know how to set challenging learning goals for themselves	+ Recognize the tools and resources that would help them find, structure and remember new information	+ Organize resources and tools to facilitate learning
+ Know how to sustain the effort and resilience that reaching those goals will require	+ Know how to transform new information into meaningful and useable knowledge	+ Monitor their progress
+ Monitor and regulate emotional reactions that would be impediments or distractions to their successful learning		+ Recognize their own strengths and weaknesses as learners
		+ Abandon plans and strategies that are ineffective

Figure 8.1. Expert learners. (From © CAST, 2012. Used with permission. All rights reserved.)

practice is to develop your students into expert learners. According to CAST (2014), an expert learner is:

- Resourceful and knowledgeable—able to activate background knowledge to identify, organize, prioritize, and assimilate new information

- Strategic and goal directed—able to devise plans and effective strategies and skilled at monitoring progress to optimize their learning

- Purposeful and motivated—able to self-regulate, set challenging learning goals, and sustain effort and resilience toward achieving mastery

Figure 8.1 illustrates the characteristics of expert learners.

How Do I know If I'm an Expert Learner?

Expert learners know what they know, understand how they learn, and are motivated to learn more. They may not be the smartest person in the room or pass every test with flying colors, and they may not know more about a subject than anyone else. They are experts at their own learning who realize that it is a process of continual change and growth (Meyer et al., 2014).

 **Reflection**

How well do you know yourself as a learner? Jot down three thoughts you have about how you learn.

Self-Reflective Learners

Every teacher and student has the capacity to become an expert learner given the right balance of challenge and guidance. A key aspect of expert learners is self-reflection. This means that they are metacognitive about their learning, setting ambitious goals and assessing their progress continually. Intentionally applying the UDL principles in your lesson planning—especially providing options for executive functioning—is a crucial step in promoting student self-reflection. To develop into a self-reflective learner yourself and to promote self-regulation among your students:

- Focus on learning why content is important to know and when and where it can be applied

- Concentrate on techniques that identify meaningful patterns of information, that highlight relationships, and that make connections between big ideas

- Create ways to assess progress, continually reviewing learning goals and adjusting effort as needed

> The only person who is educated is the one who has learned how to learn and change.
>
> —Carol Rogers, American psychologist

DEVELOPING EXPERTISE

What's the difference between experts and everyone else? You'll recall that Molly took copious notes and that Brenda just listened as Daryl explained his UDL lesson planning process. Molly asked many questions; Brenda didn't ask any. Instead, Brenda synthesized what Daryl said and reflected her summaries back to Daryl to check on the accuracy of her understanding. Molly is still developing a vision of her practice, needing to understand each new piece and evaluate it. Brenda is a veteran practitioner who's skilled at lesson planning. Her task while listening to Daryl was to find UDL nuggets that she could add to what she was already doing. Both Molly and Brenda are developing their expertise, but they are at different points along the novice-to-expert continuum. One aspect to think about as you reflect on your lessons, as you work with fellow educators who are striving to become UDL experts, and as you evaluate your students' progress is that the progression from novice to expert is based on an accumulation of experiences. It takes time.

Novice-to-Expert Scale

There are five stages to becoming an expert: 1) novice, 2) advanced beginner, 3) competent, d) proficient, and e) expert (Dreyfus & Dreyfus, 1986). Let's briefly review these stages as they apply to UDL lesson planning.

Novice   A novice needs rules or protocols to follow and is unlikely to violate those rules, even in a different context or situation. Everything has equal importance. They proceed in an overt step-by-step fashion. When a lesson is unsuccessful, they tend to blame the process or the UDL framework itself as being insufficient. Remember that Molly got confused and gave up.

Advanced Beginner   After accumulating some experience, novices become advanced beginners when they start to realize that rules are situational. They tend to focus on the details. They ask a lot of *how* questions: "How do I _____?" For instance, in an attempt to understand how to apply UDL in different situations, Daryl's friend Mike pelted him with a series of questions about how UDL would work for this student or that one.

Competent   With more experience, teachers achieve a level of competence when they are able to prioritize portions of their lessons based on their perceived importance. They use a hierarchical procedure for making decisions and need an organizational structure and plan for changing what they're currently doing. They productively engage in problem solving and can be emotionally invested in the choices they make. As an example, before making any changes to her lesson plan structure, Nicki asked Daryl to work with her to develop a plan for how she could begin to use UDL in her lesson planning.

Proficient   When teachers are able to apply intuition, balanced by calculative decision making to their lesson planning, they achieve a proficient level. They attribute success to their planning. For instance, Ben didn't ask Daryl for advice. He bought a book on UDL, selected what he thought were the important things to know, and restructured his lesson planning process by himself. He was quite proud of his success and pleased that he was doing it on his own.

Expert   With significant experiences, teachers achieve the level of an expert when they become fluid in their knowledge, performance, and decision making without an obvious awareness of their process. As experts, they perform without reflecting on every piece. They consider alternatives and are critical of their own assumptions. Daryl certainly is a UDL expert. Because Brenda is an expert teacher, she approached applying UDL to her lesson planning as an expert would.

HOW DO I KNOW IF I AM AN EXPERT?

Bransford and his colleagues (2000) summarized characteristics of expert teachers. Let's see how many of these characteristics you feel you possess:

- Experts notice features and meaningful patterns, which helps them recognize significant differences in student skills.

- Experts know a great deal about their subject matter and organize their thinking around big ideas, which can facilitate problem solving.

- Experts understand the relevance of their content, and they can guide students to learn when and why to apply concepts and when not to.

- Experts can retrieve information without much effort, which allows them to simultaneously do other things with greater ease.

 **Reflection**

Does being a subject matter expert make it easier to apply UDL to your lesson plans?

REFLECTING ON YOUR LESSON

Educators make dozens of decisions while lesson planning. Some they make quickly or on the spot; some they contemplate for a long time. It's impractical to reflect on all of those decisions. At first, take a broad perspective in your lesson reflections. What worked well? What didn't? What evidence do you have to confirm your conclusions? A more expansive reflection process includes these four overview questions:

- What happened? (Description)

- Why did it happen? (Analysis and interpretation)

- So what? (Meaning and application)

- Now what? (Implications for action)

    (See York-Barr, Sommers, Ghere, & Montie, 2001.)

Reflecting on Student Work

Those general reflection questions just mentioned are good to start with; but to engage in a deeper, more results-oriented lesson reflection process, you need to review student work for evidence of learning. As discussed in Chapter 4, there are numerous ways to assess your students' learning to determine the effectiveness of your UDL lesson, including your formative and summative lesson assessments. Reviewing this information is a critical step.

In reality, examining student work during your reflection serves two purposes: 1) to evaluate and grade student performance and 2) to answer your questions about your lesson planning process.

So, what are your questions? The best way to formulate questions about the effectiveness of your UDL lesson is to go back to your lesson's learning goal. Examining the goal will confirm the specific content you expected to share with your learners and what level of performance you anticipated from them. You can also use the UDL principles to analyze your lesson's effectiveness. Based in part on the UDL principles, Table 8.1 suggests questions to help you reflect on the impact of your lessons.

In addition to student work, other data resources can enhance your lesson reflection. You may be interested in one or more of these strategies:

- Teacher reflection logs—Record observations and anecdotal comments about lessons in a running journal. You will be able to catalog your successes and

Table 8.1.   Examples of questions to ask about student work (based in part on the UDL principles)

Engagement	How relevant is this work to the learning goal?
	What evidence is there to demonstrate that the students valued this work?
	To what extent does this work illustrate productive collaboration?
	Did the students have sufficient time to finish this work?
	Did the students stick with the tasks even in the face of barriers and mistakes?
Representation	How does this work demonstrate a clear understanding of the content?
	What does this work tell you about how these students think and learn?
	What new perspectives are evident in this work?
	To what extent does this work make connections with previous work?
	How well did the students identify patterns, critical features, big ideas, and relationships?
Action and Expression	What do you see in this student's work that was interesting or surprising?
	To what extent does this work illustrate appropriate planning?
	How effectively did the students apply tools and media?
	How much independence is evident in this work?
	To what extent did the students need, rely on, or choose to use scaffolds or models?

questions over time and determine your progress. Consider using a digital notebook or blog to make it portable.

- Daily audio snapshots—Use your cell phone or other device to periodically make an audio note on your observations. You may be so busy during the day, taking the time to sit and write notes to yourself could be too much to ask, but picking up your cell phone and recording a "Note to self" to review later might be very doable.

- Lesson videos—Again, use your cell phone or small camera or ask a colleague to occasionally video a lesson for reflection purposes. You can miss information in the midst of an experience that you can later uncover in a video. Note: Be careful. Don't post it to any public sites without written permission of every individual who's in the video.

- Learner surveys—Ask your students to complete short surveys not only of what they learned but also of how they felt during your lesson. Emotion charts, exit tickets, and quick informal classroom assessments (e.g., Fist to five; Thumbs-up/thumbs-down) are good examples.

- Learning partners—Enlist colleagues to join you. Meeting regularly with a work study team can make the UDL lesson planning journey enjoyable and enhance your learning. This topic is discussed in more depth later in this chapter.

GUIDING LEARNER SELF-REFLECTION

Research shows that students who are able to personalize learning goals are more motivated to learn (Brophy, 2004; Dean et al., 2012); however, many learners don't know how to set appropriate goals for themselves. They will need you to model relevant goal setting, providing them with models, feedback, and prompts. Use simple graphic organizers, graphs, checklists, or digital tools for student self-reflection. Blogs, class wikis, online journals, and backchannels are just a few suggestions to consider. Other suggestions for building learner self-reflection include:

- Providing opportunities for students to develop personal learning goals at the beginning of a lesson

- Presenting sentence starters for goal statements (e.g., "I can _____"; "I want to know how to _____"; or "I will _____" sentence prompts)

- Setting up data collection and analysis systems that students can keep track of themselves (e.g., progress charts or goal sheets in individual work folders or binders)

- Using KWL charts at the beginning of units or lessons, with learners completing the L-section (what did you learn) as a summary at the end

- Asking students to complete a SWOT assessment (see Chapter 1 Check-In) to guide them in identifying the strengths, weaknesses, opportunities, and threats that learning about a unit topic offers them

- Developing personal learning contracts or learning plans at the beginning of the year or term that you and the students review during periodic conference sessions

- Giving clear, productive, timely, mastery-oriented feedback

 Learning Link

To understand how to offer learners feedback that encourages a growth mindset, see Carol Dweck's web site: http://mindsetonline.com/whatisit/about/index.html.

REFLECTING WITH PARTNERS

Let's pause and explore how partner or group reflection can enhance your lesson reflection. Research has shown that discussion with a partner or as a member of a coteaching team can boost the impact of your lesson reflection, because others may see things you don't see and understand situations in different ways. Frankly, the best professional learning I ever experienced was as a member of a collaborative preschool team.

Perhaps you're reading this book as a member of a PLC. Collaborative team learning, such as that of PLCs, is a powerful staff development approach and a potent strategy for improving your teaching. Typically, a PLC consists of a group of educators who work together to improve their professional knowledge and practice with the expressed goal of maximizing student learning (Hall & Hord, 2001; Hall & Simeral, 2008; Hord, 1997). PLCs aim to create instructional environments that are focused on continuous improvement. They often use an inquiry process to review the data from rigorous student progress monitoring and formative assessments. DuFour (2004) identifies the following three big ideas for PLC members:

• Their fundamental purpose is to ensure all students learn at high levels, and members are committed to become lifelong learners themselves to make this a reality.

• Teachers and administrators work together within a culture of collaboration and interdependence.

• Members focus on results and judge their effectiveness based on evidence that students are learning.

UDL PROFESSIONAL LEARNING COMMUNITIES

In recent years, I've had the opportunity to work with dynamic PLCs focused on UDL rather than a subject area—that is, PLCs where UDL is the language of collaboration for these teams (Ralabate et al., 2014). UDL-PLCs use the UDL framework to leverage their knowledge of student learning needs and effective instruction to work in complementary ways, enhancing each other's practice. They offer dynamic, interactive ways to learn more about how to design lessons aligned with the UDL framework.

If you aren't a member of a UDL-PLC, you may want to start one. By applying the UDL principles to their lesson planning and their lesson reflection, these educators work together to:

• Develop flexible, SMART goals

• Anticipate possible learning barriers and plan for learner variability

• Assess student learning in meaningful ways

• Apply instructional methods that build understanding and scaffold learning

• Integrate media meaningfully

• Create inclusive, dynamic, effective learning environments

• Promote each other's professional growth

Whatever way you choose to reflect on your lessons, you will change how to think about your practice and how you view your instruction simply by applying the six steps of the UDL lesson planning process outlined in this book.

 **Reflection**

How will you infuse UDL into your lesson planning process? What will your next step be?

SUMMARY

Educators who apply the UDL framework successfully to their lesson planning must become expert learners (i.e., resourceful and knowledgeable, strategic and goal directed, purposeful and motivated) to achieve mastery. Everyone can become an expert learner, but not all expert learners are experts. There is a difference. According to Dreyfus and Dreyfus (1986), there are five stages to becoming an expert: novice, advanced beginner, proficient, competent, and expert. Experts notice features and meaningful patterns; what they know is organized around big ideas; they understand the relevance of their content, when and why to apply concepts; and they can retrieve information without much effort.

Developing expertise requires an accumulation of experiences and takes time. In many ways, how you reflect on your UDL lesson planning can depend on your level of expertise. Taking a broad perspective might be your first step. Try asking: "What worked well?" "What didn't?" and "What evidence do I have to confirm my conclusions?" To reflect more deeply, examine your lesson's goal and then use the UDL principles to analyze your lesson's effectiveness. Collaborating with a partner, as a member of a team of coteachers, or as a member of a PLC is a powerful way to increase the impact of your lesson reflections. PLCs that focus on learning about UDL are particularly effective.

As you apply the six steps of the UDL lesson planning process this book describes, you'll not only improve your understanding of UDL; you'll also enrich your practice. If you're ready to take the first step, UDL lesson planning expertise is at your fingertips.

CHECK-IN

UDL Lesson Planning Expertise

Using Figure 8.2, evaluate your current expertise in applying UDL to your lesson planning process. Where do you fall on the novice-to-expert scale?

UDL LESSON PLANNING IN ACTION

To learn more about reflection, the sixth and final step in the UDL lesson planning process, you may want to view a brief video (approximately 3 minutes in length). (See Video 8.1: Using Self-reflection and UDL [go online to see the video].) You'll meet Daryl, Molly, and Brenda—school colleagues who are part of a professional learning team focused on UDL. They are all expert learners who enhance their teaching expertise through self-reflection.

In this video, you'll see educators 1) recording their observations and anecdotal comments in a teacher reflection log or running journal, 2) using a cell phone or other device to periodically make an audio note on lesson observations, 3) videotaping a lesson for reflection purposes, 4) surveying students about what they've learned or how they feel about their learning, and 5) learning together as part of a professional learning team.

UDL LESSON PLANNING EXPERTISE

UDL Lesson planning expertise	Novice	Advanced beginner	Competent	Proficient	Expert
I can define flexible, SMART learning goals.					
I can take a variability perspective by using the UDL Guidelines to anticipate possible learning barriers and plan for learner variability.					
I can make my lessons matter by assessing student learning in meaningful, flexible ways.					
I can employ instructional methods that build understanding and scaffold learning.					
I can select and integrate materials and media meaningfully.					
I can reflect productively on my lessons and aim for continuous improvement.					

Figure 8.2. UDL Lesson Planning Expertise.

REFLECTION QUESTIONS

1. What was surprising about the six steps of UDL lesson planning? Is it what you expected? Why or why not?

2. In what ways are the steps of UDL lesson planning challenging for you?

3. If you could change one aspect of your current lesson planning process, what would it be? Why?

4. To what extent are you a UDL expert?

5. What types of professional expertise related to UDL would you like to add to your current knowledge and skills? How would you plan to do that?

References

Bergmann, J., & Sams, A. (2012). *Flip your classroom: Reach every student in every class every day.* Alexandria, VA: ASCD/ISTE.

Black, P., & Wiliam, D. (1998). Assessment and classroom learning. *Assessment in Education: Principles, Policy and Practice, 5*(1), 7–73.

Bransford, J.D., Brown, A.L., & Cocking, R.R. (2000). Learners and learning. In *How People Learn: Brain, Mind, Experience, and School* (pp. 31–50). Washington, DC: National Academies Press.

Brookhart, S. (2013). *How to create and use rubrics for formative assessment and grading.* Alexandria, VA: ASCD.

Brophy, J. (2001). Generic aspects of effective teaching. In M.C. Wang and H.J. Walburg (Eds.), *Tomorrow's teachers* (pp. 3–15). Richmond, CA: McCutchen.

Brophy, J. (2004). *Motivating students to learn* (2nd ed.). Boston, MA: McGraw-Hill.

Bullough, R.V. (1988). *The forgotten dream of American public education.* Ames, IA: Iowa State University Press.

CAST. (2011). *UDL guidelines—version 2.0.* Wakefield, MA: National Center on Universal Design for Learning. Retrieved from http://www.udlcenter.org/aboutudl/udlguidelines

CAST. (2014). *UDL and expert learners.* Retrieved from http://www.udlcenter.org/aboutudl/expertlearners

CAST & Danielson Group. (2014). *Crosswalk between Universal Design for Learning and the Danielson Framework for Teaching.* Wakefield, MA: National Center on Universal Design for Learning. Retrieved from http://www.udlcenter.org/implementation/udl-danielson-crosswalk

Center for Universal Design. (2015). *About UD: Universal design history.* Raleigh, NC: North Carolina State University. Retrieved from http://www.ncsu.edu/ncsu/design/cud/about_ud/udprinciples.htm

Chita-Tegmark, M., Gravel, J.W., Serpa, M.D.B., Domings, Y., and Rose, D.H. (2012). Using the Universal Design for Learning Framework to support culturally diverse learners. *Journal of Education, 192*(1), 17–22.

Cho, Y., & Brown, C. (2013). Project-based learning in education: Integrating business needs and student learning. *European Journal of Training and Development, 37*(8), 744–765.

Council of Chief State School Officers. (2008). *Attributes of effective formative assessment.* Washington, DC: Author.

Courey, S.J., Tappe, P., Siker, J., & LePage, P. (2012). Improved lesson planning with universal design for learning (UDL). *Teacher Education and Special Education, 20*(10), 1–21.

Dean, C.B., Hubbell, E.R., Pitler, H., & Stone, B. (2012). *Classroom instruction that works: Research-based strategies for increasing student achievement.* Alexandria, VA: ASCD.

Dolan, R.P., & Hall, T.E. (2007). Developing accessible tests with universal design and digital technologies: Ensuring we standardize the right things. In C.C. Laitusis & L.L. Cook (Eds.), *Large-scale assessment and accommodations: What works?* (pp. 95–111). Arlington, VA: Council for Exceptional Children.

Doran, G.T. (1981). There's a S.M.A.R.T. way to write management's goals and objectives. *Management Review, 70*(11), 35–36.

Dougherty, E. (2012). *Assignments matter: Making the connections that help students meet standards.* Alexandria, VA: ASCD.

Dreyfus, H., & Dreyfus, S. (1986). *Mind over machine.* New York, NY: Free Press.

Dudye.com. (n.d.). *Challenge your creativity: 77 Problem solving exercises.* Retrieved http://dudye .com/challenge-your-creativity-77-problem-solving-exercises

DuFour, R. (2004). What is a "professional learning community"? *Educational Leadership 61*(8), 6–11. Alexandria, VA: ASCD

DuFour, R., & Eaker, R. (1998). *Professional learning communities at work: Best practices for enhancing student achievement.* Bloomington, IN: National Educational Services.

Ebert, E.S., Ebert, C., & Bentley, M.L. (2011). Methods of teaching in the classroom. Education.com. Retrieved from http://www.education.com/reference/article/methods-teaching-classroom/

Fogarty, R. (Ed.). (2009). *Brain-compatible classrooms.* Thousand Oaks, CA: Corwin.

Goodwin, B. (2014). Which strategy works best? *Educational Leadership, 72*(2), 77–78.

Guskey, T.R. (2002). Professional development and teacher change. *Teachers and Teaching: Theory and Practice, 8*(3/4), 381–391.

Hall, G.E., & Hord, S.M. (2001). *Implementing change: Patterns, principles, and potholes.* Needham Heights, MA: Allyn and Bacon.

Hall, P., & Simeral, A. (2008). *Building teachers' capacity for success: A collaborative approach for coaches and school leaders.* Alexandria, VA: Association for Supervision and Curriculum Development.

Hargreaves, A., & Fullan, M.G. (2012). *Professional capital: Transforming teaching in every school.* New York, NY: Teachers College Press.

Hargreaves, A., & Fullan, M.G. (Eds.). (1992). *Understanding teacher development.* New York, NY: Teachers College Press.

Herreid, C.F. (1998). What makes a good case? Some basic rules for good storytelling help teachers generate student excitement in the classroom. *Journal of College Science Teaching, 27*(3). Retrieved from http://sciencecases.lib.buffalo.edu/cs/pdfs/What%20Makes%20a%20 Good%20Case-XXVII-3.pdf

Herrnstein, R.J., and Murray, C. (1994). *The bell curve: Intelligence and class structure in American life.* New York, NY: Free Press.

Hord, S.M. (1997). Professional learning communities: What are they and why are they important? *Issues...about Change, 6*(1). Retrieved from http://www.sedl.org/pubs/catalog/items/cha35 .html

Individuals with Disabilities Education Improvement Act (IDEA) of 2004, PL 108-446, 20 U.S.C. §§1400 *et seq.*

Janney, R., & Snell, M.E. (2013). *Modifying schoolwork: Teachers' guides to inclusive practices* (3 ed.). Baltimore, MD: Paul H. Brookes Publishing Co.

Johnson-Laird, P.N. (1998). Imagery, visualization, and thinking. In J. Hochberg (Ed.), *Perception and cognition at the century's end.* San Diego, CA: Academic Press.

Johnson, R., & Johnson, D. (2009). An educational psychology success story: Social interdependence theory and cooperative learning. *Educational Researcher, 38*(5), 365–379. Retrieved from http://www.co-operation.org/wp-content/uploads/2011/01/ER.CL-Success-Story-Pub-Version-09.pdf

Jones, K.A., Jones, J., & Vermette, P. (2009). Six common lesson plan pitfalls—Recommendations for novice educators. *Education, 131*(4), 845–864.

Kendall, J.S., Ryan, S.E., & Richardson, A.T. (2005). *The systematic identification of performance standards.* Denver, CO: McREL International. Retrieved from http://www.mcrel.org/~/media /Files/McREL/Homepage/Products/01_99/ prod28_systemperformstand.ashx

Kluth, P., & Danaher, S. (2014). *From text maps to memory caps: 100 more ways to differentiate instruction in K–12 inclusive classrooms.* Baltimore, MD: Paul H. Brookes Publishing Co.

Larkin, M. (2002). *Using scaffolded instruction to optimize learning.* ERIC Clearinghouse on Disabilities and Gifted Education, No. ED. 474 301. Arlington, VA: ERIC.

Larmer, J., & Mergendoller, J. (2010). Seven essentials for project-based learning. *Educational Leadership, 68*(1), 34–37.

Lipscomb, L., Swanson, J., & West, A. (2004). Scaffolding. In M. Orey (Ed.), *Emerging perspectives on learning, teaching, and technology.* Retrieved from http://epltt.coe.uga.edu/

MacDonald, E.B. (2013). *The skillful team leader: A resource for overcoming hurdles to professional learning for student achievement.* Thousand Oaks, CA: Corwin.

Marzano, R.J. (2009). *Designing and teaching learning goals and objectives: Classroom strategies that work.* Bloomington, IN: Marzano Research.

Marzano, R.J. (2010). *Formative assessment and standards-based grading.* Bloomington, IN: Marzano Research.

Marzano, R.J. (2012). *Becoming a reflective teacher.* Bloomington, IN: Marzano Research.

Marzano, R.J., Norford, J.S., Paynter, D.E., Pickering, D.J., & Gaddy, B.B. (2001). *A handbook for classroom instruction that works.* Alexandria, VA: ASCD.

Marzano, R.J., Pickering, D.J., & Pollack, J.E. (2001). *Classroom instruction that works.* Alexandria, VA: ASCD.

Messick, S. (1996). Validity of performance assessments. In G.W. Philips (Ed.), *Technical issues in large-scale performance assessments* (pp. 1–18). Washington, DC: U.S. Department of Education National Center for Education Statistics.

Metcalf, D., Evans, C., Flynn, H.K., & Williams, J.B. (2009). Direct instruction + UDL = Access for diverse learners: How to plan and implement an effective multisensory spelling lesson. *TEACHING Exceptional Children Plus, 5*(6), Article 2. Retrieved from http://escholarship.bc.edu /education/techplus/vol5/iss6/art2

Meyer, A., & Rose, D.H. (2005). The future is in the margins: The role of technology and disability in educational reform. In D.H. Rose, A. Meyer, & C. Hitchcock (Eds.), *The universally designed classroom: Accessible curriculum and digital technologies* (pp. 13–35). Cambridge, MA: Harvard Education Press.

Meyer, A., Rose, D.H., & Gordon, D. (2014). *Universal Design for Learning: Theory and practice.* Wakefield, MA: CAST.

Molenda, M. (2012). Individualized instruction: A recurrent theme. *TechTrends: Linking Research and Practice to Improve Learning, 56*(6), 12–14.

Moss, C., & Brookhart, S. (2009). *Advancing formative assessment in every classroom: A guide for instructional leaders.* Alexandria, VA: ASCD.

National Governors Association Center for Best Practices & Council of Chief State School Officers. (2010). *Common Core State Standards.* Washington, DC: Authors.

National Research Council. (2000). *How people learn: Brain, mind, experience, and school.* Washington, DC: National Academies Press.

Nelson, L.L. (2014). *Design and deliver: Planning and teaching using universal design for learning.* Baltimore, MD: Paul H. Brookes Publishing Co.

Novak, K. (2014). *UDL NOW! A teacher's Monday-morning guide to implementing Common Core Standards using Universal Design for Learning.* Wakefield, MA: CAST.

Palincsar, A.S., & Brown, A.L. (1984). Reciprocal teaching of comprehension fostering and comprehension-monitoring activities. *Cognition and Instruction, 1,* 117–175.

Palmer, P. (1998). *The courage to teach: Exploring the inner landscape of a teacher's life.* San Francisco, CA: John Wiley & Sons.

Pashler, H., McDaniel, M., Rohrer, D., & Bjork, R. (2008). Learning styles: Concepts and evidence. *Psychological Science in the Public Interest, 9*(3), 105–119.

Popham, W.J. (2003). The seductive allure of data. *Educational Leadership, 60*(5), 48–51.

Popham, W.J. (2008). *Transformative assessment.* Alexandria, VA: ASCD.

Popham, W.J., & Lindheim, E. (1980). The practical side of criterion-referenced test development. *NCME Measurement in Education, 10*(4), 1–8.

Quenemoen, R., Thurlow, M., Moen, R., Thompson, S., & Morse, A.B. (2003). *Progress monitoring in an inclusive standards-based assessment and accountability system (Synthesis Report 53).* Minneapolis, MN: University of Minnesota, National Center on Education Outcomes.

Ralabate, P.K. (2010). *Meeting the challenge: Special education tools that work for all kids.* Washington, DC: National Education Association.

Ralabate, P.K., Currie-Rubin, R., Boucher, A., & Bartecchi, J. (2014). Collaborative planning using Universal Design for Learning. *ASHA Perspectives, 15*(1), 26–31. Retrieved from http:// sig16perspectives.pubs.asha.org/article.aspx?articleid=1850863

Randi, J., & Corno, L. (2005). Teaching and learner variation. In L. Smith, C. Rogers, & P. Tomlinson (Eds.), *Pedagogy—teaching for learning,* British Psychological Society Monograph Series 2, Part 3 (pp. 47–69). Leicester, UK: British Psychological Society.

Rapp, W.H. (2014). *Universal design for learning in action: 100 ways to teach all learners.* Baltimore, MD: Paul H. Brookes Publishing Co.

Rose, D.H., Gavel, J.W., & Domings, Y.M. (2010). *UDL unplugged: The role of technology in UDL*. Wakefield, MA: National Center on Universal Design for Learning. Retrieved from http://www.udlcenter.org/resource_library/articles/udlunplugged

Rudner, L., & Schafer, W. (2002). *What teachers need to know about assessment*. Washington, DC: National Education Association.

Schumm, J.S., & Vaughn, S. (1995). Meaningful professional development in accommodating students with disabilities: Lessons learned. *Remedial and Special Education, 15*, 344–355.

Slavin, R. (2014). Making cooperative learning powerful: Five key practices bring out the tremendous potential of this approach. *Educational Leadership, 72*(2), 22–26.

Smith, M.K., & Smith, K.E. (2000). "I believe in inclusion, but...": Regular education early childhood teachers' perceptions of successful inclusion. *Journal of Research in Childhood Education, (14)*2, 161–180.

Sousa, D.A. (2011). *How the brain learns* (4th ed.). Thousand Oaks, CA: Corwin.

Spooner, F., Baker, J., Harris, A., Ahlgrim-Delzell, L., & Browder, D. (2007). Effects of training in Universal Design for Learning lesson plan development. *Remedial and Special Education, 28*(2), 108–116.

Stiggins, R. (1998). *Classroom assessment for student success*. Washington, DC: National Education Association.

Suskie, L. (2009). *Assessing student learning: A common sense guide*. San Francisco, CA: John Wiley & Sons.

Teaching Channel. (n.d.). *SWBAT: Communicating learner goals* [Video]. Retrieved from https://www.teachingchannel.org/videos/making-lesson-objectives-clear

Thurlow, M., Elliott, J., & Ysseldyke, J. (2003). *Testing students with disabilities: Practical strategies for complying with district and state requirements*. Thousand Oaks, CA: Corwin.

Vygotsky, L.S. (1978). *Mind in society: The development of higher psychological processes*. Cambridge, MA: Harvard University Press.

Wiggins, G. (2012). Seven keys to effective feedback. *Educational Leadership, 70*(1), 10–17.

Wiggins, G., & McTighe, J. (1998). *Understanding by design*. Alexandria, VA: ASCD.

Wiggins, G., & McTighe, J. (2005). *Understanding by design* (2nd ed.). Alexandria, VA: ASCD.

Wu, X. (2010). Universal design for learning: A collaborative framework for designing inclusive curriculum. *i.e.: Inquiry in Education (1)*2. Retrieved from: http://digitalcommons.nl.edu/ie/vol1/iss2/6

York-Barr, J., Sommers, W., Ghere, G.S., & Montie, J. (2001). *Reflective practice to improve schools*. Thousand Oaks, CA: Corwin.

Zabala, J. (2005). Ready, SETT, go! Getting started with the SETT framework. *Closing the Gap, 23*(6). Retrieved from http://www.joyzabala.com/uploads/Zabala_CTG_Ready_SETT_.pdf

Index

References to tables and figures are indicated with a *t* and *f*, respectively.